GLOBALVIEWPOINTS

Drugs

MAR 2 0 2009

Other Books of Related Interest

Opposing Viewpoints Series

Afghanistan

Gateway Drugs

Current Controversies Series

Drug Trafficking

GLOBALVIEWPOINTS

Drugs

Maria Tenaglia-Webster, Book Editor

GREENHAVEN PRESS
A part of Gale, Cengage Learning

GALE
CENGAGE Learning™

Detroit • New York • San Francisco • New Haven, Conn • Waterville, Maine • London

Christine Nasso, *Publisher*
Elizabeth Des Chenes, *Managing Editor*

© 2009 Greenhaven Press, a part of Gale, Cengage Learning.

Gale and Greenhaven Press are registered trademarks used herein under license.

For more information, contact:
Greenhaven Press
27500 Drake Rd.
Farmington Hills, MI 48331-3535
Or you can visit our Internet site at gale.cengage.com

For product information and technology assistance, contact us at

Gale Customer Support, 1-800-877-4253
For permission to use material from this text or product, submit all requests online at www.cengage.com/permissions

Further permissions questions can be emailed to permissionrequest@cengage.com

Articles in Greenhaven Press anthologies are often edited for length to meet page require-ments. In addition, original titles of these works are changed to clearly present the main thesis and to explicitly indicate the author's opinion. Every effort is made to ensure that Greenhaven Press accurately reflects the original intent of the authors. Every effort has been made to trace the owners of copyrighted material.

Cover photograph © Greg Smith/Corbis.

LIBRARY OF CONGRESS CATALOGING-IN-PUBLICATION DATA

Drugs / Maria Tenaglia-Webster, book editor.
   p. cm. -- (Global viewpoints)
   Includes bibliographical references and index.
   ISBN 978-0-7377-4152-0 (hardcover)
   ISBN 978-0-7377-4153-7 (pbk.)
   1. Drugs--Social aspects. 2. Drug abuse. I. Tenaglia-Webster, Maria.
   HV5801.D7295 2009
   362.29--dc22

                                    2008034545

Printed in the United States of America
2 3 4 5 6 7 12 11 10 09 08

Contents

Chapter 1: The Negative Consequences of the Global War on Drugs

Chapter 2: The Failure of Drug Prohibition Strategies

Chapter 3: Environmental Degradation Due to Drugs and Eradication Methods

Chapter 4: Alternative Policies to Prohibition

Chapter 5: Fighting Drugs Through Harm Reduction Strategies

Foreword

"The problems of all of humanity can only be solved by all of humanity."
—*Swiss author Friedrich Dürrenmatt*

Global interdependence has become an undeniable reality. Mass media and technology have increased worldwide access to information and created a society of global citizens. Understanding and navigating this global community is a challenge, requiring a high degree of information literacy and a new level of learning sophistication.

Building on the success of its flagship series, *Opposing Viewpoints*, Greenhaven Press has created the *Global Viewpoints* series to examine a broad range of current, often controversial topics of worldwide importance from a variety of international perspectives. Providing students and other readers with the information they need to explore global connections and think critically about worldwide implications, each *Global Viewpoints* volume offers a panoramic view of a topic of widespread significance.

Drugs, famine, immigration—a broad, international treatment is essential to do justice to social, environmental, health, and political issues such as these. Junior high, high school, and early college students, as well as general readers, can all use *Global Viewpoints* anthologies to discern the complexities relating to each issue. Readers will be able to examine unique national perspectives while, at the same time, appreciating the interconnectedness that global priorities bring to all nations and cultures.

Material in each volume is selected from a diverse range of sources, including journals, magazines, newspapers, nonfiction books, speeches, government documents, pamphlets, organization newsletters, and position papers. *Global Viewpoints* is truly global, with material drawn primarily from international sources available in English and secondarily from U.S. sources with extensive international coverage.

Features of each volume in the *Global Viewpoints* series include:

- An **annotated table of contents** that provides a brief summary of each essay in the volume, including the name of the country or area covered in the essay.

- An **introduction** specific to the volume topic.

- A **world map** to help readers locate the countries or areas covered in the essays.

- For each viewpoint, an **introduction** that contains notes about the author and source of the viewpoint explains why material from the specific country is being presented, summarizes the main points of the viewpoint, and offers three **guided reading questions** to aid in understanding and comprehension.

- **For further discussion** questions that promote critical thinking by asking the reader to compare and contrast aspects of the viewpoints or draw conclusions about perspectives and arguments.

- A worldwide list of **organizations to contact** for readers seeking additional information.

- A **periodical bibliography** for each chapter and a **bibliography of books** on the volume topic to aid in further research.

- A comprehensive **subject index** to offer access to people, places, events, and subjects cited in the text, with the countries covered in the viewpoints highlighted.

Global Viewpoints is designed for a broad spectrum of readers who want to learn more about current events, history, political science, government, international relations, economics, environmental science, world cultures, and sociology—students doing research for class assignments or debates, teachers and faculty seeking to supplement course materials, and others wanting to understand current issues better. By presenting how people in various countries perceive the root causes, current consequences, and proposed solutions to worldwide challenges, *Global Viewpoints* volumes offer readers opportunities to enhance their global awareness and their knowledge of cultures worldwide.

Introduction

"We find many things to which the prohibition of them constitutes the only
temptation." —William Hazlitt, nine-
teenth-century English writer

Historians know that mind-altering substances have ex-
isted since the beginning of the written word. Throughout history, cultures have struggled with substance abuse. In
Consuming Habits: Drugs in History and Anthropology, Andrew
Sherratt writes that "the availability of psychoactive products
is a constant temptation to 'misuse' . . . in the sense of an un-
restricted (and possibly habit-forming) hedonism. Few cultures allow this privilege to more than a fraction of their
members." Early on, civilizations prevented abuse through cultural and religious influences, which controlled demand, but
as trade and globalization caused demand control to falter, the
approach gradually transformed into government-led prohibition efforts to control supply instead.

In the ancient world, and into the first millennia AD, substance abuse was not widespread and was controlled by local
customs. Trade was limited, and typically, a civilization only
had access to drugs produced domestically. Opium, for example, was traditionally used as medicine for a variety of ailments only in India, and recreational use was not common.
Likewise, in the Mediterranean, wine was an integral part of
ancient Greek and Roman culture, limited to consumption
during meals and rituals, but citizens frowned on excessive
drunkenness.

More powerful than cultural traditions, religious mandates
appeared in the seventh century. Nations embracing Islamic
law recognized abstention as a key tenet. The Qur'an states
the following: "They ask you [Muhammad] about intoxicants
and games of chance. Say: In both of them there is a great sin

and means of profit for men, and their sin is greater than their profit." Even in modern times, Islamic leaders interpret this as a ban on all psychoactive substances. Later, in 1484, Pope Innocent VIII prohibited hashish. Today, the Catholic Church still maintains an official position against alcohol and drugs.

Europe entered the Age of Exploration starting in the fifteenth century, bringing increased global trade with the discovery of the New World. Christopher Columbus brought tobacco to Europe, and Spanish explorers encountered coca in South America. Drugs soon spread into India and China. For the first time, drugs were traded internationally on a large scale—purely for recreational use. Dangers soon became apparent to leaders. In Europe, Constantinople, and Japan, governments enacted laws against tobacco use. In Russia, the Czar Alexis punished tobacco use with torture in 1634.

Some subcultures continued to control drug misuse through religious teachings. Strict members of the protestant reformation, for example, adhered to temperance. According to Ruth Engs in "Protestants and Catholics: Drunken Barbarians and Mellow Romans," protestants lived in a "social psychology system with a focus on self-restraint and self-regulation." However, this marked the beginning of a time when such measures would no longer be sufficient to control drug use in the majority population.

While the global economy continued to emerge, some of the same drug-related issues we continue to struggle with today materialized, such as the conflicting interests of drug producers and drug buyers, and the difference between medicinal and nonmedicinal substance use. Around 1773, the British East India Company—recognized by many historians as the first drug cartel—discovered that opium could be sold commercially in great quantities at a high profit to recreational users. By the 1830s, the British company had a thriving business, especially in China, which was on the verge of being consumed with opium addiction. This led the British to establish opium cultivation restrictions in India—not to discourage use of the drug, but to monopolize production. This was committed to law in the Opium Acts of 1857 and 1878.

As the drug trade spread to the newly formed United States, the country struggled to protect its citizens by curtailing supply and establishing laws. The 1800s brought opium, the opiate morphine, and cocaine to physicians and consumers. Alcohol, marijuana, and tobacco were already part of the economy. As the addictive nature and dangers of these drugs became apparent, states began to enact laws. In 1860, Pennsylvania instituted the first law against morphine, and in the 1870s and 80s, California pursued a series of ever-tightening restrictions on the sale and use of nonmedicinal opium. With the United States' influence, a group of Christian missionaries convinced the British government to investigate, and eventually outlaw, its own opium trade beginning in 1893. In 1909, the United States again used its influence, this time to help China through the process of opium reform, including setting up a Chinese anti-opium commission.

The twentieth century brought heavy legislation in the face of increasing drug availability. As each new drug was discovered or became popular, its production and consumption were criminalized. Federal laws gradually replaced state laws against morphine, opium, cocaine, and heroin. European countries generally followed suit. The 1920s and 30s saw the criminalization of cannabis and the hemp plant, a previously important crop for the United States. Other drugs such as amphetamines, barbiturates, and psychedelics faced a similar rise in popularity and descent into illegality. The United Nations (UN) organized international cooperation among governments to control the drug supply by policing drug trafficking channels and encouraging nations to prohibit drug trade and use.

Not all criminalization was effective, as evidenced during the prohibition of alcohol. Many countries implemented prohibition laws in the early 1900s, including Canada, Russia and the Soviet Union, Norway, Finland, and the United States. Success in reducing consumption was negligible, and after long periods of popular protest, governments repealed the laws. Without popular support and complicity, controlling the supply was expensive and futile.

The "War on Drugs" officially began in 1971 when President Richard Nixon famously declared illicit drugs as "America's public enemy number one." Nixon, along with other politicians who came after him, believed that stemming the flow of drugs through prohibition and criminalization would help crime subside. Governments in the 1970s and 80s continued their attempts to control supply in an effort to curtail abuse and its associated ills.

In June 1998, as the UN was holding a special assembly on global drug issues, Kofi Annan, secretary general, received a letter addressing the failures of prohibition. "We believe that the global war on drugs is now causing more harm than drug abuse itself," the letter stated. Signed by a number of influential politicians and leaders from around the world, it publicly signaled growing discontent with the U.S.-led and UN-backed war on drugs. The UN did not act on the letter, and a decade later, similar policies still dominate international law.

Global Viewpoints: Drugs examines current issues surrounding the ongoing war on drugs. The authors investigate its successes and failures, along with its consequences to society and the environment. They also explore current drug control policies and consider how various countries are moving away from hard-line prohibition and experimenting with alternative measures such as decriminalization and harm reduction. While drug addiction poses one of the greatest threats to our society, many would argue that the drug war itself has also produced many dangerous consequences. The international community must now address both problems simultaneously to bring an end to this crisis.

GLOBALVIEWPOINTS

CHAPTER 1

The Negative Consequences of the Global War on Drugs

The Failure of the War on Drugs: An Overview

Ethan Nadelmann

In the following viewpoint, Ethan Nadelmann argues that the global war on drugs has failed and should end. He maintains that prohibition has been a costly mistake that drives production. Legalization and harm reduction, he argues, are better strategies. Nadelmann is a former Princeton University political science professor, and his works are widely published. He founded the Lindesmith Center in 1994, which later merged with the Drug Policy Foundation to become the Drug Policy Alliance where Nadelmann is currently executive director.

As you read, consider the following questions:

1. According to Nadelmann, why is drug control unlike disease control?

2. Which country accounts for approximately 90 percent of the world's opium supply?

3. How would the legalization of drugs benefit addicts, as explained by Nadelmann?

A "drug-free world," which the United Nations [U.N.] describes as a realistic goal, is no more attainable than an "alcohol-free world"—and no one has talked about that with a straight face since the repeal of Prohibition in the United

Ethan Nadelmann, "Think Again: Drugs," *Foreign Policy,* September/October 2007. www.foreignpolicy.com. Reproduced by permission.

States in 1933. Yet futile rhetoric about winning a "war on drugs" persists, despite mountains of evidence documenting its moral and ideological bankruptcy.

The Global War on Drugs Cannot Be Won

When the U.N. General Assembly Special Session on drugs convened in 1998, it committed to "eliminating or significantly reducing the illicit cultivation of the coca bush, the cannabis plant and the opium poppy by the year 2008" and to "achieving significant and measurable results in the field of demand reduction." But today, global production and consumption of those drugs are roughly the same as they were a decade ago; meanwhile, many producers have become more efficient, and cocaine and heroin have become purer and cheaper.

It's always dangerous when rhetoric drives policy—and especially so when "war on drugs" rhetoric leads the public to accept collateral casualties that would never be permissible in civilian law enforcement, much less public health. Politicians still talk of eliminating drugs from the Earth as though their use is a plague on humanity. But drug control is not like disease control, for the simple reason that there's no popular demand for smallpox or polio. Cannabis and opium have been grown throughout much of the world for millennia. The same is true for coca in Latin America. Methamphetamine and other synthetic drugs can be produced anywhere. Demand for particular illicit drugs waxes and wanes, depending not just on availability but also fads, fashion, culture, and competition from alternative means of stimulation and distraction. The relative harshness of drug laws and the intensity of enforcement matter surprisingly little, except in totalitarian states. After all, rates of illegal drug use in the United States are the same as, or higher than, Europe, despite America's much more punitive policies.

The Demand for Drugs Cannot Be Reduced

Reducing the demand for illegal drugs seems to make sense. But the desire to alter one's state of consciousness, and to use psychoactive drugs to do so, is nearly universal—and mostly not a problem. There's virtually never been a drug-free society, and more drugs are discovered and devised every year. Demand-reduction efforts that rely on honest education and positive alternatives to drug use are helpful, but not when they devolve into unrealistic, "zero tolerance" policies.

"The better approach is not demand reduction but 'harm reduction.'"

As with sex, abstinence from drugs is the best way to avoid trouble, but one always needs a fallback strategy for those who can't or won't refrain. "Zero tolerance" policies deter some people, but they also dramatically increase the harms and costs for those who don't resist. Drugs become more potent, drug use becomes more hazardous, and people who use drugs are marginalized in ways that serve no one.

The better approach is not demand reduction but "harm reduction." Reducing drug use is fine, but it's not nearly as important as reducing the death, disease, crime, and suffering associated with both drug misuse and failed prohibitionist policies. With respect to legal drugs, such as alcohol and cigarettes, harm reduction means promoting responsible drinking and designated drivers, or persuading people to switch to nicotine patches, chewing gums, and smokeless tobacco. With respect to illegal drugs, it means reducing the transmission of infectious disease through syringe-exchange programs, reducing overdose fatalities by making antidotes readily available, and allowing people addicted to heroin and other illegal opiates to obtain methadone from doctors and even pharmaceutical heroin from clinics. Britain, Canada, Germany, the Netherlands, and Switzerland have already embraced this last option. There's no longer any question that these strategies decrease drug-related harms without increasing drug use. What blocks expansion of such programs is not cost; they typically save taxpayers' money that would otherwise go to criminal justice and health care. No, the roadblocks are abstinence-only ideologues and a cruel indifference to the lives and well-being of people who use drugs.

Reducing the Supply of Drugs Is Not the Answer

Reducing supply makes as much sense as reducing demand; after all, if no one were planting cannabis, coca, and opium, there wouldn't be any heroin, cocaine, or marijuana to sell or consume. But the carrot and stick of crop eradication and substitution have been tried and failed, with rare exceptions, for half a century. These methods may succeed in targeted locales, but they usually simply shift production from one region to another: Opium production moves from Pakistan to Afghanistan; coca from Peru to Colombia; and cannabis from Mexico to the United States, while overall global production remains relatively constant or even increases.

> *"The United States has succeeded in constructing an international drug prohibition regime modeled after its own highly punitive and moralistic approach.... Rarely has one nation so successfully promoted its own failed policies to the rest of the world."*

The carrot, in the form of economic development and assistance in switching to legal crops, is typically both late and inadequate. The stick, often in the form of forced eradication, including aerial spraying, wipes out illegal and legal crops alike and can be hazardous to both people and local environments. The best thing to be said for emphasizing supply reduction is that it provides a rationale for wealthier nations to spend a little money on economic development in poorer countries. But, for the most part, crop eradication and substitution wreak havoc among impoverished farmers without diminishing overall global supply.

The global markets in cannabis, coca, and opium products operate essentially the same way that other global commodity markets do: If one source is compromised due to bad weather, rising production costs, or political difficulties, another emerges. If international drug control circles wanted to think strategically, the key question would no longer be how to reduce global supply, but rather: Where does illicit production cause the fewest problems (and the greatest benefits)? Think of it as a global vice control challenge. No one expects to eradicate vice, but it must be effectively zoned and regulated— even if it's illegal.

U.S. Drug Policy Should Not Be the World's Drug Policy

Looking to the United States as a role model for drug control is like looking to apartheid-era South Africa for how to deal with race. The United States ranks first in the world in per capita incarceration—with less than 5 percent of the world's population, but almost 25 percent of the world's prisoners. The number of people locked up for U.S. drug-law violations has increased from roughly 50,000 in 1980 to almost 500,000 today; that's more than the number of people Western Europe locks up for everything. Even more deadly is U.S. resistance to syringe-exchange programs to reduce HIV/AIDS both at home and abroad. Who knows how many people might not have contracted HIV if the United States had implemented at home, and supported abroad, the sorts of syringe-exchange and other harm-reduction programs that have kept HIV/AIDS rates so low in Australia, Britain, the Netherlands, and elsewhere. Perhaps millions.

The Taliban Seeks to Exploit Resentment of Eradication

In late April [2007] at the height of poppy-growing season, a team of more than 200 police officers from Kabul led by contractors working for the American company DynCorp International arrived in Uruzgan [Afghanistan] to undertake the first eradication efforts. . . . After some tense negotiations with local officials, the teams went out to begin destroying the poppy fields. . . . When the work was getting underway in earnest, a Taliban-led force bearing small arms, rocket-propelled grenades and mortars . . . attacked the eradication teams as they destroyed the fields. . . .

The Uruzgan attack demonstrated . . . just how the Taliban is seeking to exploit popular resentment against eradication efforts. All across the country, Afghan support for poppy cultivation is on the upswing. . . . In Uruzgan's neighboring province, Helmand—which supplies about half the world's opium . . . favorable ratings for the Taliban now run as high as 27 percent.

Peter Bergen and Sameer Lalwani,
"The War on Poppies,"
Los Angeles Times, September 2, 2007.

And yet, despite this dismal record, the United States has succeeded in constructing an international drug prohibition regime modeled after its own highly punitive and moralistic approach. It has dominated the drug control agencies of the United Nations and other international organizations, and its federal drug enforcement agency was the first national police organization to go global. Rarely has one nation so successfully promoted its own failed policies to the rest of the world.

[In 2007], for the first time, U.S. hegemony in drug control is being challenged. The European Union is demanding rigorous assessment of drug control strategies. Exhausted by decades of service to the U.S.-led war on drugs, Latin Americans are far less inclined to collaborate closely with U.S. drug enforcement efforts. Finally waking up to the deadly threat of HIV/AIDS, China, Indonesia, Vietnam, and even Malaysia and Iran are increasingly accepting of syringe-exchange and other harm-reduction programs. In 2005, the ayatollah [religious leader among Shiite Muslims] in charge of Iran's Ministry of Justice issued a *fatwa* [religious edict] declaring methadone maintenance and syringe-exchange programs compatible with *sharia* (Islamic) law. One only wishes his American counterpart were comparably enlightened.

Afghan Opium Eradication Is Not the Answer

It's easy to believe that eliminating record-high opium production in Afghanistan—which today accounts for roughly 90 percent of global supply, up from 50 percent ten years ago—would solve everything from heroin abuse in Europe and Asia to the resurgence of the Taliban.

But assume for a moment that the United States, NATO [North Atlantic Treaty Organization], and [Afghan President] Hamid Karzal's government were somehow able to cut opium production in Afghanistan. Who would benefit? Only the Taliban, warlords, and other black-market entrepreneurs whose stockpiles of opium would skyrocket in value. Hundreds of thousands of Afghan peasants would flock to cities, ill-prepared to find work. And many Afghans would return to their farms the following year to plant another illegal harvest, utilizing guerrilla farming methods to escape intensified eradication efforts. Except now, they'd soon be competing with poor farmers elsewhere in Central Asia, Latin America, or even Africa. This is, after all, a global commodities market.

And outside Afghanistan? Higher heroin prices typically translate into higher crime rates by addicts. They also invite cheaper, but more dangerous, means of consumption, such as switching from smoking to injecting heroin, which results in higher HIV and hepatitis C rates. All things considered, wiping out opium in Afghanistan would yield far fewer benefits than is commonly assumed.

"Legalization would strip addiction down to what it really is: a health issue."

So what's the solution? Some recommend buying up all the opium in Afghanistan, which would cost a lot less than is now being spent trying to eradicate it. But, given that farmers somewhere will produce opium so long as the demand for heroin persists, maybe the world is better off, all things considered, with 90 percent of it coming from just one country. And if that heresy becomes the new gospel, it opens up all sorts of possibilities for pursuing a new policy in Afghanistan that reconciles the interests of the United States, NATO, and millions of Afghan citizens.

Legalization Might Be the Best Approach

Global drug prohibition is clearly a costly disaster. The United Nations has estimated the value of the global market in illicit drugs at $400 billion, or 6 percent of global trade. The extraordinary profits available to those willing to assume the risks enrich criminals, terrorists, violent political insurgents, and corrupt politicians and governments. Many cities, states, and even countries in Latin America, the Caribbean, and Asia are reminiscent of Chicago under [Prohibition Era gangster] Al Capone—times fifty. By bringing the market for drugs out into the open, legalization would radically change all that for the better.

More importantly, legalization would strip addiction down to what it really is: a health issue. Most people who use drugs are like the responsible alcohol consumer, causing no harm to themselves or anyone else. They would no longer be the state's business. But legalization would also benefit those who struggle with drugs by reducing the risks of overdose and disease associated with unregulated products, eliminating the need to obtain drugs from dangerous criminal markets, and allowing addiction problems to be treated as medical rather than criminal problems.

No one knows how much governments spend collectively on failing drug-war policies, but it's probably at least $100 billion a year, with federal, state, and local governments in the United States accounting for almost half the total. Add to that the tens of billions of dollars to be gained annually in tax revenues from the sale of legalized drugs. Now imagine if just a third of that total were committed to reducing drug-related disease and addiction. Virtually everyone, except those who profit or gain politically from the current system, would benefit.

Some say legalization is immoral. That's nonsense, unless one believes there is some principled basis for discriminating against people based solely on what they put into their bodies, absent harm to others. Others say legalization would open the floodgates to huge increases in drug abuse. They forget that we already live in a world in which psychoactive drugs of all sorts are readily available—and in which people too poor to buy drugs resort to sniffing gasoline, glue, and other industrial products, which can be more harmful than any drug. No, the greatest downside to legalization may well be the fact that the legal markets would fall into the hands of the powerful alcohol, tobacco, and pharmaceutical companies. Still, legalization is a far more pragmatic option than living with the corruption, violence, and organized crime of the current system.

Wholesale legalization may be a long way off—but partial legalization is not. If any drug stands a chance of being legalized, it's cannabis. Hundreds of millions of people have used it, the vast majority without suffering any harm or going on to use "harder" drugs. In Switzerland, for example, cannabis legalization was twice approved by one chamber of its parliament, but narrowly rejected by the other.

Elsewhere in Europe, support for the criminalization of cannabis is waning. In the United States, where roughly 40 percent of the country's 1.8 million annual drug arrests are for cannabis possession, typically of tiny amounts, 40 percent of Americans say that the drug should be taxed, controlled, and regulated like alcohol. Encouraged by Bolivian President Evo Morales, support is also growing in Latin America and Europe for removing coca from international anti-drug conventions, given the absence of any credible health reason for keeping it there. Traditional growers would benefit economically, and there's some possibility that such products might compete favorably with more problematic substances, including alcohol.

The global war on drugs persists in part because so many people fail to distinguish between the harms of drug abuse and the harms of prohibition. Legalization forces that distinction to the forefront. The opium problem in Afghanistan is primarily a prohibition problem, not a drug problem. The same is true of the narco-violence [violence by drug cartels] and corruption that has afflicted Latin America and the Caribbean for almost three decades—and that now threatens Africa. Governments can arrest and kill drug lord after drug lord, but the ultimate solution is a structural one, not a prosecutorial one. Few people doubt any longer that the war on drugs is lost, but courage and vision are needed to transcend the ignorance, fear, and vested interests that sustain it.

The Afghan Poppy War Is Fueling an Insurgency

Simon Jenkins

In the following viewpoint, Simon Jenkins argues that the United States-led war on drugs in Colombia, while often perceived as a success, has been futile. He maintains that the opium war will certainly fail in Afghanistan, empowering the insurgency and creating resentment. Jenkins believes that Western-enforced prohibition only drives demand and feeds the production of narcotics. The war in Afghanistan will be more costly, resulting in wasted spending and casualties, he warns. Sir Simon Jenkins is a British newspaper columnist and a former editor of the Times *newspaper. He received a knighthood for services to journalism in 2004.*

As you read, consider the following questions:

1. According to Jenkins, what does prohibition do for the drug market?
2. How many different countries have troops in Kabul, according to Jenkins?
3. Why is it futile to train Afghan troops to fight the local militias, as explained by Jenkins?

[In February 2007], NATO [North Atlantic Treaty Organization] defence ministers met in Seville to review the

Simon Jenkins, "America Is Doped up in Colombia for a Bad Trip in Afghanistan," *The Sunday Times* (London), February 11, 2007. www.timesonline.co.uk. Reproduced by permission.

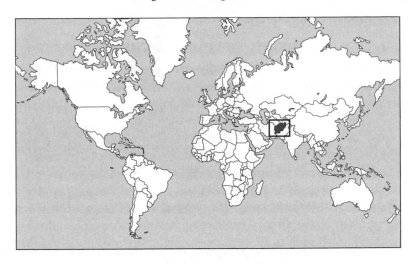

coming spring offensive in Afghanistan. . . . The new NATO commander, U.S. General John Craddock, asked for 2,000 more troops. Just one more push and the Taliban would be defeated, the Afghan army readied to fight, the opium dealers arrested and more aid committed to reconstruction. It was as simple as that. . . .

How does this strategy look from the other place in the world where it is being tried, Colombia? This month Washington is redeploying one of its star diplomats, William Wood, from Bogotá to Kabul with the enthusiastic blessing of the Pentagon. Wood has been overseeing Plan Colombia, President Clinton's eight-year effort to fight the cocaine cartels and left-wing insurgents and make Latin America safe for pro-Americanism.

Wood will be joining the new U.S. NATO commander in Kabul, General Dan McNeill, and reversing the allegedly feeble policies of the outgoing British commander, General David Richards. The fourfold increase in violence over the past year is attributed by the Americans to an excess of soft hearts and minds. Wood will want to beef up poppy eradication to starve the insurgency of revenue.

Colombia Now Safer

Colombia is undeniably a country which, six years ago [in 2001], faced disaster. Main roads were blocked by mafiosi and kidnappings and massacres were endemic. Drug lords, revolutionaries and right-wing paramilitaries fought for control of a trade that supplied 90 percent of America's cocaine. The Cali and Medellin [drug] cartels offered to finance public services and pay off Colombia's foreign debt in return for quasi-recognition by [the capital] Bogotá. This admirably capitalist innovation—de facto legalising supply—was too much for the Americans.

Instead, Washington pumped $600m a year into Colombia's army and police, enabling the central government to reestablish a measure of command over its own country. An independent, Alvaro Uribe, was elected president in 2002 and hurled men and money at security. The murder rate fell by a third and kidnappings by two thirds. Most of Colombia is now as safe as anywhere in Latin America. Uribe was reelected last year with 82 percent of the vote in a fair election.

Uribe cannot stem the cocaine trade. Crop-spraying shifts production into Bolivia, Peru and the Amazon jungle, where mile upon mile of virgin forest is lost to coca each year, an ecological disaster that is a direct result of western drug policy. As long as prohibition sustains a lucrative market for narcotics, countries such as Colombia will supply it. Traditional coca-growing nations on the Andean spine will have their politics and economics blighted by criminality. Growth will be stifled and governments left vulnerable to left-wing rebellion. The war on drugs is the stupidest war on earth.

The best that elected leaders such as Uribe can hope for is to establish a desperate equilibrium: drug suppliers kept relatively nonviolent while right-wing vigilantes are half-tolerated to counterbalance left-wing guerrillas. The only test is survival and as long as Uribe survives America smiles. On an increasingly rabid anti-American continent, he is one sure ally.

Cut to Afghanistan. Here, too, the West is intervening in a narco-economy that is destabilising a pro-Western government. Here, too, quantities of aid have been dedicated to security yet have fed corruption. Here, too, intervention has boosted drug production and stacked the cards against law and order. This year's Afghan poppy crop is predicted to be the largest on record. European demand has boosted the price paid for Afghan poppies to nine times that of wheat. At this differential a policy of crop substitution is absurd.

United States Attempts to Apply Colombia's Successes to Afghanistan

Afghanistan is not Colombia. Here the West is not using a local government to implement its drugs and counter-insurgency policy. Some 40,000 NATO troops from more than thirty different countries are gathered in Kabul. Since many of them refuse to fight, the city has become a holiday camp for the world's military elite. Outside the capital, military occupation acts as a recruiting sergeant for insurgency, leaving NATO bases constantly on the defensive. The war in Afghanistan is proving that an enemy can be held at bay but only at vast expense in money and casualties. It will not be defeated.

The British policy of occupying small towns to win hearts and minds has been a bloody failure. It was wisely replaced last autumn with deals struck with local power brokers, the so-called Musa Qala and Helmand protocols. Up to $5m is handed over to any war lord who can claim provincial control, accepting the pragmatism of the Afghan president, Hamid Karzai, who on January 29 even called for negotiation with the Taliban. The local British commander, Brigadier Jerry Thomas, was explicit in seeking to "empower local people to use traditional tribal structures . . . to find an Afghan solution to an Afghan problem". In truth, there is no other conceivable way to disengage from this mess. A similar "endgame" is being

pursued by the new American commander in Iraq, General David Petraeus, in securing safe areas policed by local militias.

Now the Americans wish to reverse British realpolitik. To them what Afghanistan needs is a taste of Colombia and Ambassador Wood.

"Poisoning Afghanistan's staple crop and contaminating fields and water supply will push up the price of opium and further breed hatred of the occupation."

Musa Qala must be reoccupied and poppy spraying must commence. This defies the view of western intelligence in Kabul which has been convinced that America's heavy-handed tactics and addiction to aerial bombardment have cost the West five years in Afghanistan. Local commanders are equally opposed to the opium eradication that obsesses the defence ministry in London and the Foreign Office's Kim Howells. Apart from the futility of trying to spray so vast an area as

Helmand, drug lords are the only counterweight to the Taliban. Poisoning Afghanistan's staple crop and contaminating fields and water supply will push up the price of opium and further breed hatred of the occupation; it is madness.

In Colombia, the Americans achieved a sort of equilibrium because local politics was left to police the narco-economy. In Afghanistan, Karzai is treated as an American puppet whose authority outside Kabul depends entirely on occupying forces. There is no way that provincial Afghanistan will be pacified by NATO and left to Karzai's army. Afghan troops (like the Iraqis) will not fight local militias. Training them to do so is pointless as they merely switch sides when the occupiers depart. Ask the few journalists brave enough to visit the battlefields of Helmand and the Pakistan border.

"Punishing supply is not a 'parallel' policy to curbing demand, as economically illiterate policy makers pretend."

In Colombia, the central government enjoyed sufficient democratic legitimacy for its army to drive insurgents into the jungle and induce the drug lords and paramilitaries to surrender (some of) their guns and power, albeit at a heavy cost in justice and human rights. Afghanistan has never enjoyed such central authority, except briefly under the Taliban. It will not do so under the guns of thirty occupying powers. The south of the country craves security and gets only bombs and bullets and is increasingly inclined to the iron rule of the Taliban. Since any prospective Karzai/Taliban coalition is unlikely to please the Tajiks and other tribes of the north, all Western meddling will achieve is to set Afghanistan on the road back to the 1990s.

Limiting Supply Will Not Curtail Demand

Having visited both Afghanistan and Colombia, I have no doubt that those countries' miseries start and end in narcotics.

With an almighty and bloodthirsty effort, the production of cocaine in Colombia and opium in Afghanistan might possibly be displaced, but only to other benighted countries. What would be the point? As long as rich countries consume these substances in massive quantities, it is hypocritical to lay waste to the poor countries producing them and thus make them poorer.

Punishing supply is not a "parallel" policy to curbing demand, as economically illiterate policy makers pretend. Demand is never curbed by limiting supply, since supply responds to price. It just will not work.

Hence pretending to victory in Colombia is no different from staving off defeat in Afghanistan. Both are cruel expiations of Western narco-guilt. The difference is that in Afghanistan intervention has led us into an unwinnable war.

Mexico's Plight Worsens Despite Military Intervention in the War on Drugs

The Drug Reform Coordination Network

*Violence continues to escalate in Mexico, despite military sup-
port sent in by President Felipe Calderón to help fight drug trafficking organizations. The following viewpoint examines how
and why military occupation in border towns is hurting the
economy and resulting in many serious human rights issues. The
Drug Reform Coordination Network is an international organization working for drug policy reform in hopes of ending drug
prohibition. The organization was founded in 1993 by executive
director David Borden.*

As you read, consider the following questions:

1. As explained in the following viewpoint, why are victims
   reluctant to report abuses from the "narcos"?
2. Why is the planned border wall causing problems for
   landowners, and why might it fail to control the border?
3. According to arguments presented by both Marco Davila
   and Juan Manuel Cantú in the article, what would help
   curtail violence on both sides of the Lower Rio Grande
   Valley?

The Drug Reform Coordination Network (DRCNet), "No Relief in Sight: Reynosa,
Mexico, Military Occupation Yields No Let-Up in Drug War Violence," *Drug War
Chronicle*, no. 523, February 15, 2008. http://stopthedrugwar.org. Reproduced by per-
mission.

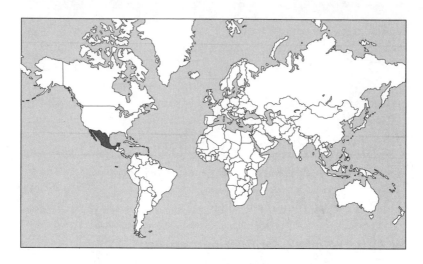

In the latest move in his ongoing war against Mexico's powerful and violent drug trafficking organizations—the so-called cartels—President Felipe Calderón [in January 2008] sent some 6,000 Mexican soldiers and federal police into the cities on his side of the Lower Rio Grande Valley, from Nuevo Laredo down to Matamoros. They disarmed the municipal police forces, who are widely suspected of being in the pay of the traffickers, established checkpoints between and within cities, and are conducting regular patrols in Reynosa and elsewhere.

A Violent Year for Border Towns

The crackdown on the Tamaulipas border towns came after a bloody year last year. According to the Reynosa-based Center for Border Studies and the Protection of Human Rights (CEFPRODHAC), drug prohibition-related violence claimed sixty-seven lives in Tamaulipas border towns last year. But it was only after a violent shootout in Rio Bravo (between Reynosa and Matamoros) [in January 2008] that resulted in several traffickers killed and nearly a dozen soldiers wounded, and the cartel's retaliatory attacks on army patrols in the center of Reynosa the next day that Calderón sent in the soldiers.

Since then, the military occupation has put a damper on the economy—and especially the nightlife—of Reynosa and other valley border towns, but it hasn't stopped the killing. According to CEFPRODHAC, as of Tuesday, [February 12, 2008] eighteen more people have been killed in the Tamaulipas drug wars so far this year, accounting for the vast majority of the twenty-five killings overall. In Reynosa, a whopping twelve of the city's fourteen homicides this year were related to the drug war, including one Sunday night [February 10, 2008].

If the army hasn't stopped the killing, it has brought the city's tourist economy to a near halt. Several bar and club owners in the Zona Rosa, the tourist zone near the international bridge said they had been ordered to close at 10:00 PM by soldiers or police. They also said it barely mattered, because they weren't getting any business anyway.

"We used to have the Texans coming across to party," said one club owner who asked not to be named. "Now they don't come. They don't want to be harassed by the soldiers."

While deploying more than 20,000 troops has won Mexican President Calderón praise from the United States, it is leading to a spike in human rights abuses.

Workers in some of Reynosa's seedier industries—prostitutes, strip joint workers, pirate taxi drivers—even led a protest march two weeks ago, complaining that the occupation was making it impossible for them to earn a living. (A pair of Reynosa businessmen who absolutely declined to go on the record claimed that the march was backed by the narcos, but that is a charge that is yet unproven.)

A Rise in Human Rights Abuses

While Calderón's resort to sending in the army—more than 20,000 troops have been deployed to hotspots in the past year—has won praise in Washington and even some support among Reynosans tired of the violence, it is also leading to a spike in human rights abuses, according to CEFPRODHAC. "We have had eleven complaints of abuse filed with us since the soldiers came," said Juan Manuel Cantú, head of the group's documentation office. "One in Rio Bravo and ten here. People are complaining that the soldiers enter their homes illegally, that they torture them, that they steal things from their homes—electronic equipment, jewelry, even food. The soldiers think they're at war, and everyone here on the border is a narco, [slang, a person involved in narcotics]" Cantú complained.

CEFPRODHAC dutifully compiles and files the complaints, Cantú said, but has little expectation that the military will act to address them. The military opened a human rights office last month, but it has so far made little difference, he said. "Until now, there is no justice. When the complaints go to SEDENA [the office of the secretary of defense], they always say there are no human rights violations."

When the abuses come at the hands of the police or the military, victims or relatives will at least file complaints, even if they don't have much expectation of results. But when it comes to abuses by the narcos, the fear of retaliation is too great for the victims or their families to complain. "People don't want to talk about those crimes," said Cantú. "They won't talk to us or the official human rights organizations, they won't talk to the military, they won't talk to the federal police. They feel threatened by the narcos."

Border Security Questioned

Paired with Brownsville and McAllen on the Texas side, Reynosa, Matamoros, and the other cities on the Mexican side are part of a bi-national conurbation [an urban area comprised of cities, towns, and larger urban areas that through expansion and population have merged into one place] with a combined population somewhere around three million. (Roughly 700,000 people in the McAllen area, 400,000 in the Brownsville area, 700,000 in Matamoros, another 500,000 in Reynosa, and a few tens of thousands scattered in between). Spanish is the most commonly heard tongue on both sides of the border. While the military occupation and the drug-war violence (for the most part) is restricted to the Mexican side, the drug trade and the drug war are felt on both sides, albeit in different ways.

Mike Allen is vice-chair of the Texas Border Commission, a nongovernmental entity that seeks to represent the interest of elected officials on the Texas side of the Rio Grande. Among the commission's primary concerns are facilitating cross-border trade and fending off what it sees as bone-headed responses to concerns about security on the border.

Number one on the commission's list of complaints is the planned border wall, which is set to cut across South Texas, forcing landowners to go through distant gates to get to portions of their property beyond the fence and, according to unhappy local officials, damaging the environment without serving its stated purpose of controlling the border. Local officials and landowners are now engaged in legal battles with the Department of Homeland Security as the department threatens to exercise eminent domain to seize property for the wall.

"The reason we have so much drug trafficking here is that we have so many American citizens taking drugs."

"The wall is a huge waste of money," said Allen. "Those of us living here know that. The Mexicans will go over, under, or around it. But you have to remember that 99 percent of the people coming across that border are trying to get jobs. They're not criminals or terrorists or drug traffickers."

But some of them are, he conceded, pointing a finger at his own compatriots. "The reason we have so much drug trafficking here is that we have so many American citizens taking drugs," said Allen. "It doesn't matter what we do—the drug trafficking will continue one way or another because there is such a demand for it in the U.S."

Prohibition-Related Violence Hurting Businesses

The drug trade has not adversely affected local economics, said Allen. That is perhaps an understatement. While the Lower Rio Grande Valley has high indices of poverty, it also has gleaming office towers, numerous banks, high-end specialty stores, thrumming traffic, and gigantic shopping centers like La Plaza in McAllen, where the JC Penney's store stays open twenty-four hours a day, seven days a week, and everyone—customers and employees alike—seems to be speaking Spanish.

"We have more banks here than we have 7-11s," former DEA [Drug Enforcement Administration] agent and valley resident Celerino Castillo chuckled ruefully. "This is supposed to be a poor area, but everybody's driving Escalades."

But while the drug trade may not have hurt business along the border, the drug prohibition-related violence associated with it has—on both sides of the border. "People hear about those shootings, and they don't want to cross the bridge into Mexico," said Allen. "A lot of Americans don't want to cross into Mexico, and that means some of them won't be coming here on their way," he said.

"We've been fighting this war for 30 years, and we're worse off than when we started."

And while there is much noise about corruption in Mexico, that door swings both ways, said Castillo, who first came to public attention when he exposed U.S.-linked drug-running

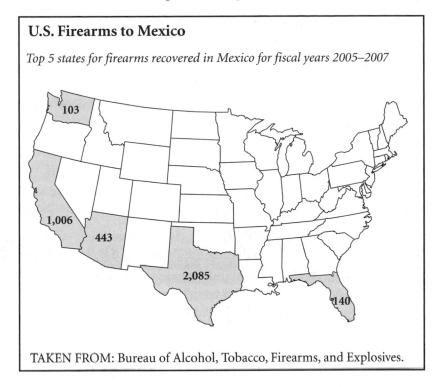

U.S. Firearms to Mexico

Top 5 states for firearms recovered in Mexico for fiscal years 2005–2007

103

1,006

443

2,085

140

TAKEN FROM: Bureau of Alcohol, Tobacco, Firearms, and Explosives.

out of El Salvador's Ilopango Air Base during the Central American wars of the 1980s in his book *Powderburns*.

"There is corruption on both sides of the border," said Castillo. "The drug war isn't about stopping drugs; it's about lining pockets. That's why this billion dollar aid package is just bullshit. We've been fighting this war for thirty years, and we're worse off than when we started."

Cartels Acquiring Weaponry Is a Growing Concern

Castillo regularly works gun shows in the area selling Vietnam-era memorabilia, and he said he regularly encounters cartel members there. "They're always showing up looking for weaponry," he said, "along with members of the Mexican military. It's very, very busy."

Some handguns are in high demand by cartel members, said Castillo. "They really like the Belgian FN Herstal P90 because they can easily remove the serial number," he explained. "These things retail for $1,000, but cartel buyers will turn around and pay $2,500 for them, and whoever takes them across the border gets $4,000 a weapon," he said.

Other, heavier weapons and munitions are not available in the civilian gun market, but that just means the cartels use other networks, Castillo said. "The heavy weapons, the grenade launchers, the mass quantities of ammo are only available in military armories, here or in Central America. We sell tons of weapons to the Salvadoran Army, and it's my belief they're turning around and selling them to the cartels."

Better Programs Needed

The drug trade thrives off poverty on both sides of the border, said one local observer. "In reality, you can put a lot of money into policing, but people have to eat, people have to survive," said Marco Davila, a professor of criminology at the University of Texas-Brownsville. "If there are no jobs, you have to do something. It's not just the drug trade, there is also prostitution, theft, and other forms of deviance."

What is needed on both sides of the Lower Rio Grande Valley is real assistance, not massive anti-drug programs for law enforcement, said Davila. "You can put that money wherever, but if the people are still hurting, it will be a toss-up whether it will work. The people who need money are not the cops and soldiers," he said.

CEFPRODHAC's Cantú agreed with that assessment. "That money isn't going to make us safe," he said. "It won't do anything good. If the soldiers get that U.S. aid, it will only mean more violence. They are prepared for war, not policing. What we need are programs for drug education and prevention, even here in Mexico, but especially in the United States," he said. When asked about drug legalization, Cantú was willing to ponder it. "It might stop the violence," he mused.

Poverty Driving Drug Trafficking

On the Texas side, said Davila, a culture of poverty traps whole generations of poor Latinos. "Look at these kids in Brownsville," he said. "They have no hope. They've given up. They're not talking about trying hard. They're saying 'We're gangsters, we're gonna sell drugs.' People used to have tattoos of the Virgin [Mary, Roman Catholic icon venerated in Mexico] of Guadelupe, but now she's been replaced by [Al Pacino's gangster character in the 1983 film] *Scarface*."

On the other side of the river, poverty drives the drug trade, too—as well as illegal immigration. "The Mexicans are just broke, scared, and hungry. They have nothing else," said Davila. "If they don't want to go into an illegal trade, like drug trafficking, they come across the border any way they can. People are putting their lives on the line to cross that river," he said.

And many of them are paying the ultimate price. According to reports from Reynosa human rights watchers, seventy-five would-be immigrants drowned in the Rio Grande between Nuevo Laredo and Matamoros last year. Another five have drowned already this year.

And so it goes on the Mexican border. Just as it has for the past twenty years, when in yet another stark example of the law of unintended consequences, then-President Reagan appointed Vice President George Bush to head a task force designed to block Caribbean cocaine smuggling routes. From that moment, what had previously been relatively small, local, family smuggling operations carrying loads of marijuana into the United States began morphing into the Frankenstein monster known as the cartels.

Mexico and the United States are inextricably intertwined. A solution to the problems of drug abuse and the violent black market drug trade is going to have to be a joint solution. But few observers on the ground think throwing more money at Mexico's drug war is the answer.

The Colombian Paramilitary Presence Is Still a Threat Despite Drug War Efforts

Vanda Felbab-Brown

Opponents of United States intervention in Colombia argue that anti-drug aid only feeds the corrupt military and police linked to terrorist groups. In this viewpoint, Vanda Felbab-Brown questions the current demobilization strategy in Colombia. Despite some success, there are growing concerns that demobilized paramilitary groups have resurfaced while new groups steadily emerge. The United States should have full disclosure of the connections between Colombia's politicians and the paramilitaries that depend on drug profits, argues Felbab-Brown. Furthermore, police should be protecting the population and challenging paramilitary efforts. Felbab-Brown is a professor at Georgetown University and a former research fellow at the Belfer Center for Science and International Affairs at Harvard University.

As you read, consider the following questions:

1. According to Felbab-Brown, how and when did paramilitaries originate in Colombia?
2. What was President Álvaro Uribe's offer of leniency, as explained by the author?
3. According to Felbab-Brown, how do the paramilitaries continue to influence the political process?

Vanda Felbab-Brown, "What President Bush Needs to Ask President Uribe," The Brookings Institution, March 9, 2007. www.brookings.edu. Reproduced by permission.

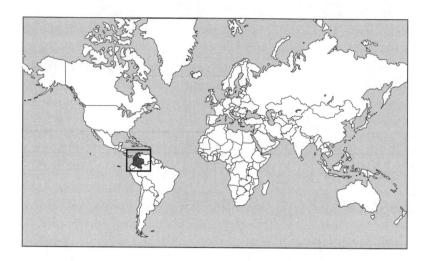

On his visit to Colombia [in March 2007] rewarding President Álvaro Uribe for his compliance with the U.S. war on drugs and for being a staunch U.S. supporter in an otherwise antagonized Latin America, President Bush should raise some tough questions about the demobilization of Colombia's paramilitaries. He should also stress the need for a more complete—geographic and functional—extension of the Colombian state.

Following his election in 2002, President Uribe negotiated the disarmament of the rightist paramilitary groups that by then had become a major independent force, taking over territory, fighting the leftist guerrillas (the [Revolutionary Armed Forces of Colombia] FARC and the [National Liberation Army] ELN), trafficking in drugs, and engaging in wholesale massacres and intimidation of the population. The paramilitaries originated as private defense militias of cattle ranchers and landowners against the guerrillas as far back as the 1960s and as bodyguards of the drug lords of the 1980s. Under the leadership of Carlos Castaño [founder of the Peasant Self-Defense Forces of Colombia (ACCU)] during the 1990s, they coalesced under an umbrella organization [the United Self-Defense Forces of Colombia (AUC)] and vastly grew in number.

But ironically, an impetus for the paramilitaries' expansion and growth in power was the destruction of the Medellín and Cali drug cartels in the mid-1990s. The fragmented boutique drug cartels left in the wake of law enforcement successes against the large cartels were vulnerable to the paramilitaries takeover and also in need of the paramilitaries' protection. From the drug traffickers' perspective, the relationship with the paramilitaries was easier than with the leftist guerrillas. Moreover, the paramilitary units battling the leftist guerrillas were frequently tolerated by the military, once again an advantageous situation for the traffickers. In the late 1990s, many more or less independent drug traffickers bought themselves positions of power in the paramilitary umbrella organization to cloak themselves with political legitimacy.

"There is increasing evidence that many of the demobilized paramilitaries continue to operate para-state structures, intimidate the population, and engage in criminal activities, including drug trafficking."

Violence Decreasing as Paramilitaries Demobilize

Facing extradition charges on drug trafficking counts to the United States, the paramilitaries took up President Uribe's offer of leniency: no extradition to the United States, no more than eight years in prison, and the seizure of their assets proven to have been acquired illegally in exchange for demobilizing their units, handing over their weapons, and ending their drug trafficking ventures. In fact, as of now, over 30,000 have officially demobilized and over fifty of the top commanders are in prison in Itagüí. Massacres against the population have decreased dramatically as the paramilitaries' role in the conflict decreased. These are important accomplishments.

Still, despite the seeming success, there are tough questions to be asked about the demobilization of the paramilitaries. In

51

principle, there is nothing wrong with leniency and amnesty and, in fact, this method has been an important part of ending violence and civil wars in many places—in Italy during the era of the [1970s Italian Terrorist Group] Red Brigades, in Malaya during the 1960s, and in Peru's struggle against the [Communist Party] Shining Path during the 1990s, to name just a few. Colombia itself has a long history of negotiating with both rebels and criminals, although the success rate there is much lower. Many of the leftist guerrillas who demobilized under an amnesty scheme during the 1980s and formed a political party were gunned down by the paramilitaries, deterring others from negotiations since. Colombia's negotiations with key drug traffickers, such as Pablo Escobar, put some of them for a while in jail, but they continued running their smuggling operations from there, and the deal ultimately broke down.

Paramilitaries Continue to Undermine Government

Issues of justice aside, major questions remain about the efficacy of the process. There is increasing evidence that many of the demobilized paramilitaries continue to operate para-state structures, intimidate the population, and engage in criminal activities, including drug trafficking. They may not be walking around in uniforms and with AK-47s [assault rifles] any more and instead carry silencers on their Rugers [branch of firearm] but they maintain a strong and frequently violent grip on large parts of Colombia, such as the Atlantic Coast and parts of Medellin. New paramilitary groups are emerging and continuing to battle the leftist guerrillas over drugs and territory. The paramilitaries also continue to influence the political process through violently intimidating, killing, and buying off opposition at the local and regional level. Over the past months, the Uribe government has been rocked by revelations of the paramilitary alliances with his top political supporters

Links Between Armed Groups and Drugs Are Complex

The Colombian and U.S. governments are convinced that fighting drug production and trafficking are essential elements of a security policy that can defeat the armed groups or bring them to negotiate in a position of relative weakness. However, while links between the armed groups and the drug business are obvious and deep—dating back to the 1980s—they are far from clear-cut or simple.

Not only has this relationship changed profoundly over the past fifteen years, but there are also stark differences between the drug roles of the [Revolutionary Armed Forces of Colombia] FARC, the [United Self-Defense Forces of Colombia] AUC and the [National Liberation Army] ELN— even within the groups and between the regions of the country. The ELN is less involved and obtains the bulk of its illegal funding through kidnapping and extortion. The AUC and FARC, who extract significant amounts of money from the trade, maintain a strong presence in all zones where coca and opium poppy are cultivated, run armed monopolies by imposing the price of coca base on the peasant-cultivator, control the routes by which chemical precursors, coca or cocaine, guns and ammunition are smuggled, and often exchange coca/cocaine for guns. The AUC and FARC also hand out "licenses" to cocaine refining laboratories and tax members of the drug cartels, who buy the cocaine and traffic it to the United States and Europe.

International Crisis Group,
"War and Drugs in Colombia,"
International Crisis Group:
Latin America Report No. 11, *January 27, 2005.*

and members of congress. Even a less visible paramilitary presence will continue to undermine any future negotiations with the guerrillas, expose the critical weakness of the Colombian state, and ultimately delegitimize it.

President Bush should demand a full disclosure of the connections between the paramilitaries and Colombia's politicians, not simply at the national level, but also at the local and regional level where ultimately the connection between the population and the state is made and where legitimacy and authority of the state is created. He also needs to demand that the police that President Uribe placed throughout the country in fact protect the population and challenge the resurgent paramilitaries instead of guarding each other. Finally, a major effort must be given to reintegration of the demobilized paramilitaries in Colombian society, so that they do not again end up as criminals and para-fighters.

Periodical Bibliography

The following articles have been selected to supplement the diverse views presented in this chapter.

Diego Cevallos — "UN-backed War on Drugs a Failure in Mexico," *Inter Press Service* (IPS), December 27, 2007.

Drug Policy Alliance Network — "What's Wrong With the Drug War?" 2008. www.drugpolicy.org.

Cindy Fazey — "International Policy on Illicit Drug Trafficking: The Formal and Informal Mechanisms," *Journal of Drug Issues*, October 1, 2007.

Misha Glenny — "The Lost War," *The Washington Post*, August 19, 2007.

Jim Hoagland — "Poppies vs. Power in Afghanistan," *The Washington Post*, December 23, 2007.

Human Rights Watch — "Not Enough Graves: The War on Drugs, HIV/AIDS, and Violations of Human Rights in Thailand," 2006. www.hrw.org.

Richard Lapper, Anastasia Maloney et al. — "At War with the Law of Supply and Demand," *Financial Times* (London), January 14 2008. www.ft.com.

Allan Massie — "'War on Drugs' Can Never Be Won—and It Is Folly to Pretend It Can," *The Scotsman*, December 13, 2007.

Ethan Nadelmann — "Mexico President Calderón Should Not Repeat Drug War Failures of the Past," *The Huffington Post*, March 1, 2007. www.huffingtonpost.com.

Neal Peirce — "Drug War's Latest Achievement: Boosting Global Terrorism," *The Seattle Times*, September 4, 2007.

Peter Reuter — "What Drug Policies Cost. Estimating Government Drug Policy Expenditures," *Addiction*, no. 101, 2006, pp. 312–322.

GLOBALVIEWPOINTS

CHAPTER 2

The Failure of Drug Prohibition Strategies

A Long History of Failure with Prohibition: An Overview

Alfred W. McCoy

In the following viewpoint, Alfred W. McCoy takes a historical look at prohibition as a failed policy. He argues that prohibition efforts stimulate both drug production and consumption and continue to cause many problems including damage to the environment, military strife, human rights violations, and the spread of HIV. Alfred W. McCoy is a history professor at the University of Wisconsin-Madison and has written extensively on Southeast Asian history and politics. His 1972 book, The Politics of Heroin, *initially roused controversy; however, now in its third edition and translated into nine languages, it is regarded as a world-renowned source on Asian drug trafficking.*

As you read, consider the following questions:

1. What were the long-term consequences of President Richard Nixon's drug war, according to McCoy?

2. According to McCoy, how did United Nations suppression contribute to an AIDS epidemic in Thailand?

3. As argued by McCoy, what are some possible risks associated with opium eradication efforts in Afghanistan?

Alfred W. McCoy, "The Stimulus of Prohibition: A Critical History of the Global Narcotics Trade," *Dangerous Harvest: Drug Plants and the Transformation of Indigenous Landscapes*, Oxford: Oxford University Press, 2004, pp. 94–97. Copyright © 2004 by Oxford University Press, Inc. All rights reserved. Reproduced by permission of Oxford University Press, Inc.

Clearly, there are reasons to question the effectiveness of the current prohibition effort. Perfect coercion has proven effective over the past two centuries, but imperfect coercion has unleashed a whirlwind of unforeseen consequences. With their near perfect coercion, European colonial empires were able to promote cultivation where needed (India) and suppress it where not (Southeast Asia), fostering a commodity trade that was by the late nineteenth century integrated into the global economy.

The Consequences of Coercion

In the twentieth century, global drug prohibition has produced more ambiguous results. In the last half of the last century, the most dramatic development was China's use of coercion, within a closed society, to effect a total eradication of all opium production and use after 1949. Judging by this success, perfect coercion can effect a major reduction in drug trafficking. However, China's experience is historically unique and might not be relevant to the more open political systems that have emerged since 1989. Indeed, China itself has recently experienced a sudden surge in drug trafficking as it lessened social controls during the 1990s to encourage development.

Outside the socialist bloc, the League of Nations, and later, the United Nations, have attempted a prohibition on legal opium sales, at first producing a sharp but short-term decline in both drug production and consumption. But from the start of drug prohibition in the 1920s, criminal syndicates have emerged to link highland growers and urban addicts, creating a global illicit market. A half century later, President [Richard] Nixon's forceful intervention in this illicit market produced another round of unintended consequences. Through bilateral coercion, his drug war [the term "drug war" was first used by Nixon] crippled the Mediterranean opium traffic, uprooting poppy fields in Turkey and closing heroin laboratories in Marseilles [France]. Over the longer term, however, this exercise in imperfect coercion unleashed global market forces that ultimately stimulated an increase in the supply of drugs on five continents.

How Suppression Increases Production

Market response to imperfect coercion is complex and ultimately counterproductive. Since the 1920s, the syndicate's response to suppression has been supple, sophisticated, and often capable of compromising even the best attempts at coercive intervention. Similarly, even the most effective narcotics suppression efforts can have unforeseen consequences. Over the past quarter century, it has become evident that suppression efforts, particularly bilateral initiatives, can stimulate narcotics production. Even so, the United States and the United Nations have persisted for over fifty years in a quixotic [impulsive], self-defeating strategy that defies the dynamics of the global drug market. A policy presaged on an assumption of inelastic supply cannot succeed when the market shows repeatedly that the global drug supply is surprisingly elastic. In sum, this attempt to reduce the drug supply through a policy that defies the dynamics of the illicit market has produced unanticipated, unwanted market responses—notably, steady increases in the global drug supply that has sustained rising demand worldwide.

"Eradication has stimulated both drug production and consumption."

As we saw in Turkey during the 1970s and Thailand in the 1980s, suppression, both bilateral and multilateral, can effect a dramatic short-term reduction in the drug supply that will, in succeeding crop years, encourage an increase in total global production. The success of the United Nations program in reducing Thai opium cultivation during the 1980s may well have contributed to the simultaneous increase in Burma's [officially, Union of Myanmar] poppy harvest. Moreover, by raising the price of smoking opium to addicts in Thailand, and thus encouraging the spread of intravenous heroin injection, United Nations suppression contributed to an AIDS epidemic in Thailand. Apparently, heroin supplies, when denied entry into one market, as they were in Southeast Asia during the 1970s, will seek another, resulting in a proliferation of consumption and an overall increase in global demand. Successful United Nations eradication of opium in Asia could thus stimulate a rapid spread of poppies along the Andes, just as U.S. defoliation of poppy fields in the Andes could encourage production in Asia. Should such bilateral and multilateral operations overcome myriad obstacles to effect a long-term reduction in narcotics supply, then domestic dealers, repeating the U.S. experience with amphetamines in the 1970s, could turn to the manufacture of synthetics. In effect, the eradication of both Asian opium and Andes coca could stimulate the production and consumption of chemical substitutes across the globe.

Eradication Efforts Prove Counterproductive

Any attempt at solving America's heroin problem by reducing the global opium supply through a war on drugs thus seems unrealistic. Successful bilateral eradication has, over the past quarter century, stimulated both drug production and consumption. Since America consumes a tiny share of the world's supply and pays the world's highest price, the elimination of the American heroin supply requires that illicit opium cultivation disappear from the face of the globe. In 1985, for example, the United States consumed only six tons of opium out of a worldwide harvest of 1,465 tons, just 0.4 percent of the total. In 1997, the White House estimated that the United States still consumed "only 3 percent of the world's [heroin] production." If the illicit drug traffic operates like any other market, then America's drug warriors must eradicate some 97 or 99.6 percent of the world's opium before they finally get to those last few tons destined for the high-priced U.S. market.

As we have seen from past U.S. and United Nations drug control efforts, the illicit market often reacts in unforeseen ways, transforming repression into stimulus. Before launching crop eradication or criminal suppression, anti-narcotics agencies need to consider the full range of possible outcomes. Over the past century, each attempt at prohibition has produced an unexpected market reaction that has allowed the illicit traffic to adapt, survive, and in recent years, even expand. It may be time to learn from the past and develop strategies for minimizing the negative impact of drug control efforts.

"It might be helpful to abandon the drug war rhetoric and adopt a medical metaphor of treatment and healing."

More broadly, it may be time to admit that prohibition's supply-side solution has failed. Since the first U.S. drug war in the 1970s, successful bilateral eradication has stimulated both drug production and consumption. Although U.S. and United Nations drug operations have produced a short-term decline of drug production in target societies, they have simultaneously stimulated an increase in later harvests elsewhere in Asia and the Andes. After thirty years of failed eradication, there is ample evidence to indicate that the illicit drug market is a complex global system, both sensitive and resilient, that quickly transforms suppression into stimulus. If past experience in Turkey is any guide, the possible eradication of opium in Afghanistan, through the United Nations drug program or U.S. intervention, could unleash unpredictable market forces that will ramify invisibly through the global system for years to come, contributing to a spread of narcotics production, drug consumption, HIV infection, and synthetic drugs.

The "Balloon Effect"

Current policies frequently conflict with each other and generate "unintended consequences." For example, forced eradication tends to displace plantings to new areas. This, so called, "balloon effect" means that policy success is only local but that globally, eradication might have little or no long-term effect. Furthermore, if a "balloon effect" does occur, forced eradication results in a significant "unintended" environmental damage as more old native forest is destroyed to plant new illegal crops and in some cases, large migrations to other rural and urban areas where uprooted peasants settle. Forced eradication also has the "unintended" effect of weakening community loyalty to the state, and the displacement of peasants might increase the willingness of young people to join armed groups like FARC [Revolutionary Armed Forces of Colombia]. Both of these are obstacles to achieve a long-term solution.

Francisco E. Thoumi, The Causes of Illegal Drug Industry Growth in the Andes, Anti-Drug Policies and Their Effectiveness, *2005.*

Supply Reduction vs. Demand Reduction

For thirty years or more, U.S. and United Nations drug policy has been wedded to unexamined prohibition. In its 1997 *World Drug Report,* for example, the United Nations warned of dire consequences from any relaxation of prohibition—possibly depriving farmers of their drug crops, creating unemployment among "hundreds of thousands of intermediary" traffickers, conceding political power to drug cartels, and encouraging a massive increase in drug abuse. Although admitting that demand reduction was more effective, the [United Nations Drug Control Program] UNDCP insisted on the "many notable achievements" of its supply reduction strategy, arguing that "drugs that would have appeared in the streets are being seized in ever-greater quantities" and financial controls "have the potential to inflict real harm on drug trafficking networks." Similarly, the United States has fought five major drug wars since 1971, applying localized coercion to the eradication of a global commodity. The White House has used a metaphor of war in each of these campaigns, applying the military logic of rapid-fire campaigns with fixed spatial objectives to the eradication of an elusive global commodity.

Recognizing the power of paradigms to shape concepts and thereby frame policy, it might be helpful to abandon the drug war rhetoric and adopt a medical metaphor of treatment and healing. This conceptual change could encourage a replacement of militarized prohibition with long-term global management of a complex drug market. Instead of a metaphor of war, with its rhetoric of maximum force and sudden victory, international drug policy could, in the short term, recognize the complexity of this illicit economy and intervene with the greatest of caution, realizing that every action is likely to produce an unpredictable reaction, greatly compounding the problem. As a first step, we might consider shifting resources from supply eradication to demand reduction through voluntary treatment. Narcotics control could move from the United Nations Drug Control Program to the World Health Organization, from the United States Justice Department to the Department of Health and Human Services.

The Price of Failure

Over the longer term, the international community could dismantle the prohibition apparatus built during the past century and replace it with a more cautious attempt to manage the harm from drugs—not only from the traffic itself but also, above all, from the suppression programs designed to combat it. Such change might not end the illicit traffic in drugs or the spread of consumption. But at least this more modest approach will stop governments from applying coercive measures against both highland producers and urban consumers that often do more social damage than drug use itself. . . .

Looking back on this century-long, Anglo-American experiment in drug prohibition, we need to entertain the possibility that this effort has failed—both the international suppression of supply and the domestic control of individual behavior. Over the past thirty years, prohibition has not reduced the production or consumption of illicit drugs. Moreover, the price of this failure has been extraordinarily high: extensive defoliation, forced migration, and military conflict in the source nations; mass incarceration, rising HIV infection, spreading drug use, and social polarization in the consuming countries. Invisible to the panopticon of modern media, the price that highland minorities in Asia and the Andes have paid for their involvement in narcotics production and eradication has been inhumanely high—guerrilla taxes, crop defoliation, military operations, and economic dislocation.

The Afghan Drug War Cannot Be Won Through Eradication and Prohibition

Transnational Institute

As opium production in Afghanistan is reaching record levels, pressure is rising for the international community to reduce poppy cultivation. While many drug war supporters are pushing for aerial chemical spraying and calling for foreign troops to get involved in prohibition efforts, those in opposition believe that such short-term fixes will only worsen conditions in this already war-torn country. In the following viewpoint, it is argued that none of the current policy debates takes into account the global demand for heroin. Long-term solutions and peace-building efforts are instead needed. The Transnational Institute (TNI) was founded in 1974 and is comprised of activist-scholars devoted to analyzing and promoting possible solutions to global problems.

As you read, consider the following questions:

1. As explained in the following viewpoint, why is governor-led eradication generally negotiated?
2. How can interdiction have an adverse effect on drug production?
3. As indicated, why are there unrealistic expectations for alternative livelihoods?

Transnational Institute, "Missing Targets: Counterproductive Drug Control Efforts in Afghanistan," *Transnational Institute Drug Policy Briefing No. 24*, September 2007, pp. 1–7, 9–10. www.tni.org. Reproduced by permission.

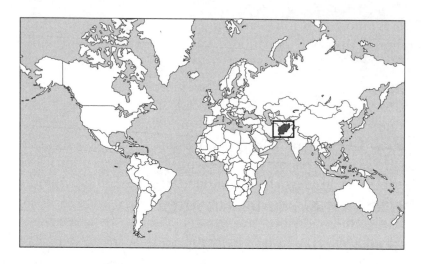

Despite efforts by the Afghan government and the international community to reduce poppy cultivation, opium production in Afghanistan has once again reached record levels in 2007. The United Nations Office on Drugs and Crime (UNODC) annual survey estimates that 193,000 hectares [unit of land equal to 100 ares, or 2.471 acres] is under poppy cultivation, a 17 percent increase on the record levels of 2006, yielding a harvest of 8,200 mt [metric tons] (an increase of 34 percent). The main policy instruments to bring down these figures—eradication of opium poppy fields and implementing alternative livelihoods projects—are missing their targets.

As a result, pressure is growing to start aerial chemical spraying of poppy fields, and calls to involve foreign troops in interdiction [prohibition] efforts are getting louder. In this briefing, TNI [Transnational Institute] argues that such over-reactions will worsen an already deteriorating security situation. Policy responses should instead be based on a better understanding of local, national and global trends in the opium/heroin market and a more sophisticated analysis of the nature of the drugs-and-conflict connections in Afghanistan today.

None of the responses dominating the public and policy debates—stepping up eradication, a focus on interdiction, more funds for alternative livelihoods or a licensing of opium production—fully take into account the reality of an existing global demand for heroin.

"It needs to be clear . . . that [alternative livelihoods] programmes alone are not going to bring about a major breakthrough in reducing opium cultivation."

The international community needs to face the reality that the entrenched illicit economy in war-torn Afghanistan will not dwindle easily, and that pursuing illusions of quick solutions will do more harm than good. As a recent report by UNODC and the World Bank warns: "While the drug industry itself constitutes a serious threat to the state-building agenda in Afghanistan, ill considered counter-narcotics actions can be counterproductive in terms of governance, possibly exacerbating an already difficult situation."

The Balancing Act

Provincial governors in Afghanistan face a difficult dilemma. [Afghan] President [Hamid] Karzai has made them responsible for reducing opium production figures in their provinces. But too much pressure on the farmers may lead to violent resistance, further decline of support for the government, and could upset the delicate tribal balance in the province. Yet if their approach is perceived to be too lenient by the central government in Kabul, it may send the U.S.-trained Afghan Eradication Force (AEF) [formerly the CPEF, Central Poppy Eradication Force] to the province, increasing the risk of conflict.

Governor-led eradication is mostly negotiated. This is both for practical reasons—the governor often does not have enough power to enforce eradication in the districts that are controlled by powerful warlords—as well as for political reasons—he does not want to lose the support of tribal leaders.

Therefore, many governors try to do a bit of eradication in all districts in order to 'spread the pain equally'. The level of eradication, therefore, also greatly differs from province to province.

By contrast, decisions about AEF deployment are made at the central level by the Ministry of Interior, in consultation with the United States Embassy in [Afghan Capital] Kabul. They are greatly resented by most governors and local district authorities. "It is a little unnerving when you get a phone call from Kabul saying we are sending the AEF up. That is a motion of no confidence," according to a Poppy Elimination Programme (PEP) team member. AEF deployments, therefore, regularly lead to violent clashes.

In order to assist the governors, PEP teams were created in seven key opium producing provinces: Badakshan, Nangarhar, Helmand, Kandahar, Balkh, Uruzgan and Farah. Each team consists of about ten Afghan staff and some international advisors. . . .

PEP teams carry out public information campaigns by visiting key poppy growing districts, organising Jirgas [assemblies, or community council meetings] with tribal leaders and local communities. They disseminate messages through radio and print media, warning farmers about the dangers to health and security of growing poppy and the risks of eradication that they face. PEP teams further aim to facilitate alternative livelihood programmes and assist the governor-led eradication campaigns. The teams also support UNODC in its task of assessing levels of poppy cultivation, and monitoring and verifying eradication activities.

Corrupted Figures

Corruption is rampant in Afghanistan and eradication campaigns are no exception. Eradication has often become a new source of income for local officials, who accept bribes from owners and sharecroppers in return for not eradicating their fields.

There are also accusations that eradication figures are inflated to gain additional income. Governors are compensated at $120 per hectare for the expenses involved in eradication verified by UNODC. According to the UNODC's methodology, "eradication verifiers are part of the governor-led eradication teams".

While in Nangarhar the verification procedure seems to work relatively smoothly and the teams are well-equipped, PEP teams and governors in some other provinces complain that UNODC lacks the capacity to effectively carry out its task and is behind schedule. Some PEP teams have, therefore, in turn, decided to 'verify' the UNODC verification process. . . .

UNODC does not verify AEF eradication. The AEF started its 2007 eradication campaign in Helmand province, and initially claimed it had eradicated 7,573 hectares. After that, the AEF moved north into Uruzgan province, where it immediately ran in to trouble. The AEF team, consisting of Afghan and U.S. security officials using tractors and all-terrain vehicles, was attacked with mortars and small arms, and four Afghan team members were wounded. The AEF subsequently withdrew and the mission was called off, having destroyed only some seventy hectares. . . .

Eradication and Interdiction

ISAF [International Security Assistance Force, a NATO-led security and development mission in Afghanistan established in 2001] troops are not directly involved in eradication. In fact, Western military forces have been reluctant to get involved in the narcotics issue at all because they fear it may endanger their mission to bring peace and stability. However, they may be called upon to assist AEF or governor-led eradication teams that are under attack.

The Afghan Eradication Coordination Cell (AECC) was set up in order to prevent a conflict of interest between AEF eradication missions and ISAF security operations. Consisting of representatives of the Ministry of Counter Narcotics and the Ministry of Interior, the AECC informs ISAF where and when it plans to carry out eradication missions. ISAF may also ask the AEF not to go into certain areas—especially in the south—if it is deemed to conflict with its own operations.

At the provincial level, the Joint Provincial Coordination Centres are supposed to coordinate between the Afghan National Army and the Afghan National Police and ISAF. However, there is no coordination mechanism for governor-led eradication campaigns with ISAF. . . .

There is growing pressure on ISAF troops to become involved in interdiction by sharing intelligence, detecting drug convoys and heroin labs, and even attacking these. "The drugs dealers, the Taliban and the warlords are the same network", says General Khodaidad, Afghanistan's Deputy Minister of Counter Narcotics. "NATO [North Atlantic Treaty Organization] should destroy these people. They should hit their headquarters, their convoys, the drugs labs and factories."

Interdiction by NATO troops is problematic, however. Few of the conflict actors in Afghanistan—including those aligned with the government—can claim to have clean hands in the drug trade, and decisions about who to arrest or attack are often politically motivated. NATO could become involved in local and tribal conflict dynamics. . . .

"Eradication and interdiction is not conflict neutral but targets political opponents, usually competing local commanders or other tribes."

Furthermore, there are doubts about the effectiveness of interdiction as a policy instrument. In some cases, interdiction may even have an adverse effect on drug production. . . . In principle, seized and destroyed quantities of opium and heroin do not lead to less consumption but are replaced by increased production. . . .

Experience in Afghanistan and in other parts of the world shows that eradication and interdiction is not conflict neutral but targets political opponents, usually competing local commanders or other tribes. The widespread corruption in the country further contributes to a focus on poor farmers and small-scale traders, driving people into the hands of anti-government insurgents. . . .

Punishing the Poor

Eradication of the Afghan opium crop has been justified by claiming it is targeted against farmers who should be able to find other means of livelihoods—what Western officials often call targeting "the greedy not the needy". According to Thomas Schweich, newly appointed U.S. coordinator for counter narcotics in Afghanistan: "We are not targeting poor farmers, this is fiction." UNODC executive director [Antonio Maria] Costa even states in the foreword to this year's survey: "Opium poppy cultivation in Afghanistan is no longer associated with poverty—quite the opposite."

"Those presently targeted by eradication . . . have the fewest alternatives available to them."

The Afghan government has stated that "eradication must target areas where alternative livelihoods exist." In order to accomplish this, the British Embassy drug team has produced socioeconomic maps with target areas eligible for eradication. These target areas are based on a number of criteria, including rural livelihood projects, distance to markets, water availability, agricultural diversity, population density, extension of government access to non-farm income and credit. Local security conditions are also included, based on ISAF assessments.

In practice, however, this targeting policy is not implemented. . . .

Instead, those presently targeted by eradication are mostly those who have the fewest alternatives available to them. . . .

Until eradication is aimed at rich land owners and government officials in the first instance, drug control activities will continue to be seen as hypocritical and corrupt and will only alienate the rural communities. Poppy cultivation continues to be intricately linked with poverty and livelihood insecurity, and the discourse about 'targeted eradication' is basically a myth.

It is no surprise that in several cases farmers have tried to resist both governor-led and AEF eradication. . . . Farmers were also reported to have resisted eradication by flooding their fields, preventing the tractors from ploughing their crops. These farmers' protests in several provinces forced eradication teams to withdraw and suspend their activities. . . .

Signed, Sealed, and Delivered

While pressure on the farmers is increasing, the efforts of the Afghan government and the international community to provide viable alternatives for poppy farmers remain woefully insufficient. There is great frustration among poppy growing communities about the lack of aid coming into their villages. "If our poppy is eradicated, we have no other possibility to live in this area", says a farmer from Argu District in Badakhshan province. "We want to know what the government is doing for us. They got a lot of money, but all they do is come here and eradicate our fields."

Provincial Governors in turn blame the central government for pressuring them to stop growing opium but without giving them the necessary resources to develop their regions. . . .

Afghan government officials have complained about a lack of funds. Former interior minister [Ali Ahmad] Jalali recently claimed that only a fraction of the estimated costs for the reconstruction of Afghanistan were provided by the international community, and that most of these funds are outside the control of the Afghan government. He also stated there is growing frustration about the slow pace of "tangible reconstruction activity".

While this may well be true, at the same time there is lack of capacity at all levels in the Afghan government to implement programmes and to absorb more aid. . . .

There are valid questions about the effectiveness of existing aid programmes. It is unclear what percentage of the funds spent on Afghanistan are actually spent in the country itself. . . .

Virtual Reality

Many actors in Afghanistan see the development of alternative livelihoods (AL) as the answer to Afghanistan's drugs problem. The alternative livelihoods approach seeks "to mainstream counter narcotics objectives into national development strategies and programmes", and is best understood as doing "development in a drugs environment". It needs to be clear, however, that AL programmes alone are not going to bring about a major breakthrough in reducing opium cultivation. AL projects are still small-scale, especially compared to the massive opium cultivation in the country.

There are unrealistic expectations of what AL programmes can actually deliver. They do not function in isolation and the success of any programme depends on the specific situation and on the dynamics of the licit and illicit markets. At best, these projects can serve as a laboratory to identify and then propagate viable alternatives to poppy cultivation. But expecting huge impacts in a growing drugs economy such as in Afghanistan is unrealistic.

It is worth continuing this experimentation, but the current scope and performance of AL programmes should in no way be used to justify claims that, since alternatives exist, eradication is, therefore, justified. Such claims are leading to

Current Counter-Narcotics Policies Are Risking Mission Failure in Afghanistan

The forced eradication of poppy crops is fuelling support for the Taliban and the insurgency, thereby compromising international troops' safety and their mission in Afghanistan; and poppy crop substitution programmes are failing Afghanistan's farming communities. Forced eradication and poppy crop substitution strategies are failing to provide Afghan farmers with access to the resources and assets necessary to phase out illegal poppy cultivation. . . .

Poppy for Medicine is an alternative counter-narcotics strategy that has been successfully implemented in many countries. It involves licensing the controlled cultivation of poppy to produce essential poppy-based medicines such as morphine, and unlicensed poppy cultivation remains a criminal activity.

Poppy for Medicine projects were established in Turkey in the 1970s with the support of the United States and the United Nations, as a means of breaking farmers' ties with the international illegal heroin market without resorting to forced poppy crop eradication. Within just four years, this strategy successfully brought the country's illegal poppy crisis under control.

The Senlis Council, "P4M: Poppy for Medicine,"
SenlisCouncil.net, 2007. www.senliscouncil.net.

huge resentment among the majority of farmers for whom AL is a virtual reality in which they play no part.

Similarly, experimenting with licit uses of opiates for medicinal purposes merits attention, but should be equally stripped of the illusion that it could bring 'solutions' in the short or medium term, as is often reported in the media with reference to Senlis Council reports. . . .

Conclusions on the Way Forward

Policy considerations based on a distorted and over-simplified analysis of the link between opium and conflict in Afghanistan threaten to exacerbate the current downward spiral. . . .

What is needed instead are conflict-sensitive drug policies that take into consideration all of the interrelations between the opium economy, conflict and reconstruction. . . .

Four different positions are competing with each other in the media as well as policy circles in the search for 'solutions': stepping up eradication, more focus on interdiction, mainstreaming of alternative livelihoods or a licensing scheme for licit opiates production. One key deficiency is that none of these options takes on board the state of existing demand for illicit heroin, a reality that cannot be wished away by good intentions of supply reduction. Illicit demand for Afghan opiates seems to be on the rise at the moment and any policy that does not incorporate this reality is suffering from self-denial.

The rural economy of Afghanistan will be heavily dependent on opium production for the foreseeable future. Likewise, the global illicit opiates market will remain heavily dependent on Afghanistan until either demand will be reduced or other production sites emerge elsewhere.

An overall conclusion is well phrased by the UNODC/ World Bank study, which states that "with modest resources and weak institutions fighting against a diverse, flexible, mobile, and dynamic drug industry, *expectations about what can be accomplished in the short run must be kept reasonable.* Overly inflated expectations—whether about eradication, other enforcement measures, or alternative livelihoods—inevitably lead to disappointments, which given the political sensitivity of narcotics in turn can lead to overreaction and policy mistakes. . . . Thus there is no alternative to a sustained long-term effort, with success inevitably being modest and elusive in the short run."

This is a particularly important point to stress at this very moment, when the newly released record figures have led to media hypes and policy panicking. Overreaction and mistakes—such as aerial spraying or a counter-narcotics mandate for NATO—have unpredictable consequences and may well further close doors to stabilisation, peace building and reconstruction.

Colombia's Eradication Policies Are in Need of Change

Chris Kraul

After several years of failed eradication efforts with "Plan Colombia," the United States Congress has begun to fund alternative development programs in hopes of encouraging farmers to grow legitimate crops and avoid joining paramilitary groups. In the following article, Chris Kraul investigates how funding such ventures in the Choco state of Colombia is helping to both curb illicit drug crops and improve the quality of life for impoverished members of the community. Chris Kraul is a staff writer for the Los Angeles Times *in Bogata, Colombia.*

As you read, consider the following questions:

1. As stated in the following article, how many dollars in United States taxpayer money has been spent on the seven-year "Plan Colombia" program to fight drug traffickers and guerrillas?

2. Why, according to Kraul, is the jagua tattoo ink project the kind of program that United States aid officials want to fund?

3. What percentage of Forest Guardian families returned to their former occupation of growing illicit crops, as cited in the article?

Chris Kraul, "U.S. Looking for 'Softer' Approach to Drug Fight," *Los Angeles Times*, October 4, 2007, p. A1. Reproduced by permission.

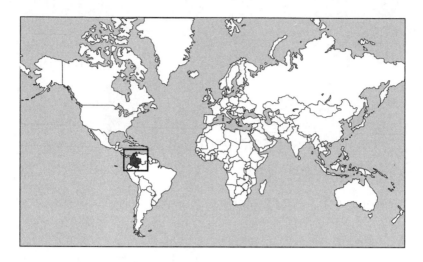

From his dugout canoe in the Napipi River [Colombia], Jefferson Rojas spotted what he was after: a 40-foot-high jagua tree, its canopy dotted with dozens of thick-skinned fruits the size of tennis balls.

Rojas pulled his boat to shore, macheted his way through thick foliage, and with his telephone lineman gear, quickly scaled the tree. He lopped off the fruits, which fell with thuds to the floor of the jungle.

> *"The 'hard' features of Plan Colombia—the spraying and military aid—have done little to stem the flow of cocaine to North America and elsewhere."*

Why did Rojas go to such lengths for a fruit that isn't even ripe? Because the body-marking market has caught on to what indigenous tribes here in Choco state have known for centuries: Jagua is an excellent source of nonpermanent tattoo ink.

Ink that eventually makes its way to the biceps or backsides of trendy teenagers thousands of miles away might appear to have a tenuous connection to Plan Colombia, the seven-year program that has funneled $5.4 billion in U.S. taxpayer money into fighting drug traffickers and guerrillas. But with the current fiscal year, which began Monday [October 1, 2007] more of those funds are to go to economic projects such as Rojas' tattoo ink venture and fewer to finance the Colombian military and anti-coca spraying than in past years.

The initiative will soon take on a "softer" profile, at the insistence of the Democratic-controlled U.S. Congress. It is expected to contain more money to fund "alternative development" programs to encourage farmers to grow legal crops and steer clear of joining armed groups.

After seven years, the "hard" features of Plan Colombia—the spraying and military aid—have done little to stem the flow of cocaine to North America and elsewhere, and members of Congress and like-minded Colombian officials want to try a new approach.

Funds Are Being Shifted to the Grassroots Level

A quarter of the approximately $550 million in annual Plan Colombia aid typically has been earmarked for economic development, justice reform and institution-building, but the percentage could grow to 40 percent next fiscal year. That means the U.S. Agency for International Development office at the U.S. Embassy in [Colombia's capital] Bogotá could see its budget balloon to as much as $218 million from this year's $139 million, said U.S. congressional staffers familiar with the appropriations process.

"It is beyond dispute that spraying chemicals is not a sustainable strategy," Sen. Patrick J. Leahy (D-Vt.), chairman of the Appropriations subcommittee controlling foreign aid expenditures, said in an e-mailed comment. "Without real economic alternatives, coca farmers will find ways to grow coca. . . . Rather than continue to act as a rubber stamp, we are shifting more funds into economic and social programs."

The jagua tattoo ink project is just the sort that aid officials will be looking to fund. It is environment-friendly, gives incentives for peasants to stay away from violence and drug trafficking, and it helps Afro-Colombian [Colombians of African ancestry] communities, which many aid critics consider a neglected constituency.

In Choco, Afro-Colombian communities such as Napipi have received about $350,000 in aid from the United States and from the Organization of American States through its Pan American Development Foundation arm.

The fruit gathered by Rojas will be peeled by other members of his cooperative in this impoverished river town of 900, and the pulp sent on charter flights to the EcoFlora factory near Medellin [largest city in Colombia after Bogotá]. The family-owned company, which sells cut flowers, extracts an inky blue liquid from the fruit and ships it in powder form to a tattoo parlor supply distributor called Primal Cosmetics in Manchester, England.

In less than a year, the venture between EcoFlora and the largely Afro-Colombian community in this remote corner of Colombia's wettest rain forest expects to generate $300,000 in sales, via Primal Cosmetics, to tattoo parlors in Britain, the United States, Australia and other countries.

EcoFlora chief executive Nicolas Cock Duque said that figure could grow significantly if plans to sell the extract as food coloring to an unnamed soft drink manufacturer come through.

The EcoFlora project provides a case study of how renewable resources can produce real economic gain in isolated, grindingly poor towns like this one.

About half of the $300,000 in revenue comes back to Napipi in wages to Rojas and thirty other cooperative members. That's a bonanza in this depressed town where people eke out subsistence living by fishing, farming and illegal logging.

Statement of Senator Patrick Leahy (D-Vt.), chairman, Senate Subcommittee on State and Foreign Operations

"The Administration and the Congress have a fiduciary responsibility to American taxpayers to use these dollars wisely and to take care that U.S. military aid is part of the solution, instead of perpetuating Colombia's problems.

"When Plan Colombia began, we were told it would cut by half the amount of cocaine in five years. Six years and $5 billion later, it has not had any measurable effect on the amount of cocaine entering our country. We need to assess what has worked, what has not worked, and what we can reasonably expect to accomplish. We want to support Colombia, and we will. But the new Congress is not going to write a blank check the way the last Congress was."

Senator Patrick Leahy,
"Statement on President Uribe's Visit and on Funding
for Plan Colombia," May 2, 2007, http://leahy.senate.gov.

Choco has been the scene of considerable strife in recent years as narco-traffickers, leftist rebels and right-wing paramilitary groups have fought over its strategic geography. Much of Colombia's estimated 500 tons of cocaine, shipped annually to the U.S., is processed in the region. More than half a dozen Napipi residents have been killed in drug and insurgent violence in recent years, locals say. In 2002, more than 100 Afro-Colombians in the neighboring town of Bojoya were killed when guerrillas engaged in fighting paramilitary forces launched mortar attacks on a church where residents had taken refuge.

Keeping Families in Legal Farming

Rojas, 27, has a wiry build and intense eyes that seem to reflect his determination to avoid the violence that has scarred his town. The idea of moving to a bigger city such as [Choco capital] Quibdo or Medellin does not interest him. He also farms beans and corn, and it's the country life he has chosen, despite the poverty and violence.

Rojas said young men in his town are tempted to join an armed group not because of ideology, but because it is one of the few ways to earn a regular salary of $200 a month or more. Having a job even as minimally remunerative [profitable] as jagua collection is a powerful incentive to "resist the proselytism [practice of conversion] of the armed groups," he said.

The jagua business also gives locals an alternative to cutting down cedar and other protected tree species in a rain forest increasingly under siege by loggers, said Juan Diego Lopez, an observer for the Pan American Development Foundation. Rojas and others also got training in how to cut the fruit to ensure future harvests.

Forest Guardians, a program monitored by the United Nations that pays Colombians formerly growing opium and coca to raise legitimate crops, currently aids about 50,000 families. The Colombian government wants to add 80,000 more by 2010.

Much of the additional U.S. development aid could go to help the Colombian government's Social Action agency finance, an expanding program called Forest Guardians, in which families that grew coca leaves and opium poppies are paid monthly stipends to raise legitimate crops. The stipends are conditional on all townspeople not replanting illicit crops and on their directing their energies to new crops and markets, such as for organic coffee and tropical fruit juices.

The program, monitored by the United Nations, aids about 50,000 families, and the Colombian government wants to add 80,000 more to the rolls by 2010.

The push is on to expand the program because it seems to be the most successful means of taking families out of illicit farming and keeping them out. Diego Molano, the assistant director of Social Action, said that only 25 percent of Forest Guardian families so far had gone back to planting illicit crops, whereas 80 percent of farmers whose coca and poppy crops had been sprayed had returned to illegal farming.

Vanda Felbab-Brown, a researcher at the Brookings Institution in Washington, said alternative development projects take decades and require unflinching commitment by government and the private sector.

"Unfortunately, on a countrywide level, alternative livelihoods projects have rarely been successful, with Thailand being the most prominent example of success," Felbab-Brown said, referring to that country's twenty-year campaign to eliminate poppy farming. "Years of sustained and well-funded effort are necessary for such efforts to bear fruit."

Options in Napipi are few. Most of the inhabitants, like Rojas, have been displaced by war and drug trafficking and, as marginalized Afro-Colombians, feel they have no place else to go.

Rojas, a much-valued member of the cooperative for his tree-climbing skills, says membership in the group is not an unalloyed positive. Rojas and others volunteered for the program, which is anything but a welfare handout. The work is strenuous and hazardous, and there isn't a time when he scales one of the three-story-tall jagua trees that he doesn't fear he'll fall. And townspeople who aren't members of the thirty-family cooperative are envious of his wage.

Still, he's happy to be earning an income.

"The economic well-being here has risen," Rojas said. "The quality of life is higher."

The United Kingdom's Failed Policy of Prohibition Yields a Criminal Justice Crisis

Transform Drug Policy Foundation

In the following viewpoint, it is argued that prohibition is a policy that has failed globally. In the United Kingdom, prohibition's collision with the rising demand for drugs has created serious problems, including a crisis in the criminal justice system and public health risks within the community. Harm reduction, the authors contend, is at odds with the current harm-maximizing prohibitionist framework. Transform Drug Policy Foundation (TDPF) is a charitable think tank seeking drug policy reform. TDPF is committed to research, policy analysis, and development that provide alternatives to the current prohibition regime.

As you read, consider the following questions:

1. According to the viewpoint, what occurs as prohibition and demand collide and drug prices inflate?
2. Why have police efforts failed to control the drug supply in the United Kingdom?
3. How much (in British pounds) is the United Kingdom's illegal drug market estimated to be worth in untaxed criminal profits?

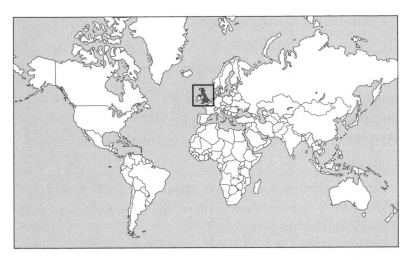

Like many failed prohibitions of the past, drug prohibition has become unworkable. Unfortunately it has survived into the twenty-first century—with disasterous results.

Prohibition—A Policy Whose Days Are Numbered

The economics of global prohibition have inflated the price of heroin and cocaine to such an extent that, by the time they reach the United Kingdom (UK), any attempt to eliminate the market domestically is futile and counterproductive. Prohibition is a failed policy, and the magnitude of the error is becoming more obvious as increased demand for illegal drugs has collided with outdated legislation that seeks to prohibit them. Thankfully, it is a failure that can be rectified. Whilst the obstacles are great, prohibition contains within it the seeds of its own destruction, its counter-productivity, making it untenable in the long term. Once the political will exists to terminate prohibition the perceived obstacles will evaporate. . . .

The collision of prohibition with rapidly rising demand for drugs has created serious problems associated with illegal drug markets, maximising drug related harms to users and the wider community.

Policy related harms include:

1. The creation of crime

2. A crisis in the criminal justice and prisons system

3. Harm maximisation for drug users

4. Political, economic and social instability...

5. Mass criminalisation and the undermining of human rights

Enforcement is either ineffective or actively counterproductive and policy related harms are now far greater than harms caused by drug misuse.

Harm reduction initiatives are largely mitigating against health harms created or exacerbated by prohibition, whilst new resources for drug treatment are primarily an attempt to reduce prohibition-related crime. Neither addresses the intractable problems associated with illegal drug production and supply....

"Prohibition has created the conditions whereby a relatively small number of problematic users are now responsible for the majority of shoplifting, burglary, theft from motor vehicles, robbery and nearly half of all fraud."

There is some evidence that prohibition can prevent the availability of commodities when demand for them is low. However, once demand is established, the effect of prohibition is to establish a high level of arbitrage between supplier and consumer, and thus, to encourage a lucrative criminal market. At this point—which we reached a generation ago—prohibition becomes a 'gangster's charter', and the original drug problem becomes subsumed into a vast criminal economy.

As the market absorbs risks, including the costs of avoiding enforcement, wholesale drug prices inflate by as much as 2000 percent. The unfortunate and unintended impact of this price hike is simultaneously to make the trade immensely attractive to organised crime and raise street prices to levels where dependent users often resort to acquisitive crime to support a habit. Even if enforcement was successfully reducing availability (which it is not) the effect would merely be to push up the price and create still more crime amongst dependent users. The more prohibition is enforced, the worse the problems get.

As demand for illegal drugs has accelerated in recent decades, organised criminals and unregulated dealers have moved to exploit the growing profit opportunity to devastating effect. The collision of laws that prohibit drug use with rapidly expanding demand for drugs has created catastrophic negative impacts that were never foreseen when the UN [United Nations] treaties were first drafted (some of the text in the 1961 UN treaty was drafted in the 1940s). Far from reducing the harms associated with drug use, prohibition has in reality maximised drug related-harms and created a crisis in our criminal justice system.

It is testimony to the failure of imagination in drug policy thinking in the thirty-five years since 1971 that it has taken such a catastrophic policy failure for the reform debate to achieve any level of visibility. On almost any measure, prohibition has been either ineffective or actively counterproductive, creating problems that were previously minimal or nonexistent. In the process the inability to acknowledge its ineffectiveness, and the glaring mismatch between the government line and reality, have been significant contributors to the loss of public trust in government.

Harms Created by Prohibition

When reviewing the effectiveness of current policy, and considering options for reform, it is important to make the distinction between the harms that result from drug misuse and the harms that are a result of policy, specifically the enforcement of prohibition. The key harms created by prohibition are:

1. Creation of Crime at All Levels

- *Organised International Criminal Gangs*: Violent criminal networks now control an international trade worth over £100 billion [British pounds] a year and a market turnover approaching £300 billion a year. Drug magnates and cartel bosses have become the Al Capones [Prohibition Era gangster] for a new generation, exploiting drug prohibition for profit and power, and located beyond the reach of the law. They are routinely involved in violence and murder, corruption, fraud, money laundering, illegal arms trading and terrorism.

- *Organised Local Criminal Gangs*: Criminal gangs battling for a share of drug profits are a significant source of antisocial behaviour and street violence in the UK. Such 'turf wars' have fuelled the alarming recent rise in gun crime, murder, assault and intimidation, making some inner city areas virtual no-go zones [neighborhood areas where police and military are restricted].

- *Acquisitive Crime*: Low-income problematic users (primarily of heroin and crack cocaine) frequently turn to offending [criminal activity] to raise money to pay the inflated price of illegal street drugs. Whilst many of these individuals may have been involved in offending before becoming problematic users, it is clear that the need to fundraise dramatically increases the intensity and volume of offences (precisely the reason that abstinence-based treatment is so central to the Government's crime reduction strategy). Prohibition has created the conditions whereby a relatively small number of problematic users are now responsible for the majority of shoplifting, burglary, theft from motor vehicles, robbery and nearly half of all fraud.

- *Prostitution*: For female problematic users with no other source of income, prostitution often becomes the most viable source of fundraising to buy drugs. The Home Office estimates that 95 percent of those involved in street soliciting are problematic users. This is the most visible and dangerous tier of sex work, and these individuals are themselves frequently victims of violence.

- *Prohibition Crimes*: Prohibition criminalises all activities involved in the production, supply, and possession of certain drugs, making criminals of a significant proportion of the population. A 2002 ICM [research company] poll found numbers of regular users of the following drugs: Cannabis 5.1 million, Ecstasy 2.4 million, Amphetamine 2.1 million, Cocaine 2 million, and Heroin 426,000. If lifetime use is included, prohibition is now criminalising one quarter of the adult population, and approaching half of all young people. These remain serious and imprisonable offences, and the accompanying criminal record has serious implications for employment, housing, travel and personal finance.

2. A Crisis in the Criminal Justice System and Prisons

- *Police Failures*: As was recently acknowledged in a report from the Number 10 Strategy Unit report, UK police enforcement efforts have had, at best, a localised, temporary and marginal effect, and failed to make any meaningful impact on illegal drug supply. In the U.S., where the war on drugs is prosecuted with unprecedented intensity, the drug market still thrives and drugs are, as in the UK, cheaper and more available than they have ever been. Police attempts to stamp out this trade have always failed precisely because it is so lucrative. With the inflated prices and extraordinary profits on offer, criminal entrepreneurs view the efforts of police and customs as an occupational risk. If there is a police crackdown in one area, the market simply moves to another. If one smuggling network is smashed, another rapidly emerges to fill the void. If one dealer is arrested, there is a queue of willing replacements. Even high security prisons are awash with drugs. When demand is high, prohibition simply cannot succeed.

- *Prison Overpopulation*: The deepening prisons crisis is fuelled by prohibition-related offending. On top of the exponential rise in the number of imprisoned drug offenders over the last decade (increasing five-fold for women and three-fold for men between 1992 and 2002) anecdotal evidence suggests that between 50 percent and 80 percent of prisoners are inside for crimes relating to fundraising to buy illegal drugs. Today, nearly half of all women in prison in the UK are there for drug offences, over half have a child under the age of 16, and nearly three quarters have had a drug problem. The UK is now the leading per capita incarcerator in the European Union.

- *Racism in the Criminal Justice System*: The discretionary nature of drug enforcement, in particular stop and search powers, has made drug enforcement a driver for prejudice and racism within the criminal justice system. In the UK, black offenders receive harsher treatment at every stage of the criminal justice process, being more likely than whites to be stopped and searched, arrested and prosecuted, and they receive longer sentences. As a result, black drug offenders are significantly over-represented in prison and prosecution statistics, despite the black community having a per-capita level of drug use lower than whites.

- *Economic and Social Costs*: A Home Office study estimated that the economic and social costs of class A drug use in England and Wales in 2000 was between £11.1–£17.4 billion. Of this total 99 percent was due to problematic users, and 88 percent (between £10–16 billion in one year) was costs of crime committed by problematic users.

- *Billions in Wasted Expenditure and Lost Tax Revenue*: Direct annual expenditure on 'tackling drugs' in the National Drug Strategy for 2002/3 was £1026 million, of which approximately two thirds was spent on enforcement. Over and above this total (on the basis of the Government statistic that a third of all crime is illegal-drug related), a significant proportion of all resources flowing into the criminal justice system, in policing, courts, prisons and probation, is now absorbed by the enforcement of prohibition and dealing with its negative consequences. The precise size of this wasted expenditure is uncounted but certainly runs into billions every year.

- The UK illegal drug market is now conservatively estimated to be worth around £6.6 billion a year in untaxed criminal profits. Others have estimated that the cannabis market alone is worth £5 billion a year. Whatever the exact figure, it is clear that substantial tax revenue, totaling billions annually, is being lost to illegal profiteers as a result of prohibition.

3. Harm Maximisation for Drug Users

- Prohibition abdicates control for drug production and supply to criminal networks, and in doing so maximising the risks associated with their use. Illegal drugs are of unknown strength and purity, contain unspecified contaminants and come with no health or safety information. The UK now has the highest level of drug related deaths in Europe.

- The risks of illegal drug use are particularly acute for injecting users with high rates of HIV infection and over a third of injectors in the UK and Wales infected with hepatitis C. Over fifty people died from a single batch of biologically contaminated heroin in 2000.

4. Political, Economic and Social Instability

- Illegal drug markets now form a significant proportion of the economies in key producer and transit countries such as Afghanistan, Colombia and Jamaica, undermining their social, economic and political stability.

- Illegal drug profits are used to corrupt officials at all levels of politics, judiciary, police and military. It is estimated that Colombian drug cartels spend more than $100 million each year on bribes to Colombian officials.

- Illegal drug profits are helping to fund and arm paramilitary groups, guerrilla groups, and terrorist organisations across the globe, fuelling violence in conflict zones.

5. Mass Criminalisation and the Undermining of Human Rights

- Only a few decades ago problematic drug users were treated in the UK for what they were—vulnerable people in need of help. Prohibition turns the majority of those without substantial private means into criminal outcasts, exacerbating social exclusion and throwing yet more obstacles in the way of achieving employment, housing, personal finance, and a generally productive and healthy life.

- Millions of otherwise law abiding individuals are being criminalised in a way that is arbitrary, unjust, and incompatible with the European Charter of Human Rights.

- There is widespread use of the death penalty for drug offences in violation of the UN Charter of Human Rights. China routinely celebrates UN world anti-drugs day with mass executions of drug offenders, sixty-four being executed on June 27th 2002, up from fifty-four the previous year. Over 2000 people have died during Thailand's drug 'crackdown' launched in 2002, many thought to be extra-judicial police executions.

- An estimated 2 million people are imprisoned globally for drug offences, one quarter of the total prison population. This places a huge financial and human cost on society with little evidence of benefits.

- Indigenous cultures in some producer countries that have long traditions of medical and ceremonial uses of local drug crops (coca, opium and cannabis) have come under attack through the criminalisation of traditional practices and aggressive eradication programmes.

- It is invariably the weakest links in the illegal drug chain (peasant growers, drug 'mules', and problematic users) who feel the greatest impact of drug enforcement. The most serious criminals have the resources to evade legal consequences and bargaining power as informants if they are caught. . . .

Prohibition Creates Offenders

Harm reduction is a concept that in any other field of social policy would be taken as a given. In drug policy, it has been adopted late and reluctantly. Progress is still hampered by the emotive political environment, as is evident by the UK Government's continuing and baffling refusal to countenance heroin consumption rooms, despite the wealth of positive evidence from mainland Europe, Australia and Canada, and support from many police and most drug agencies.

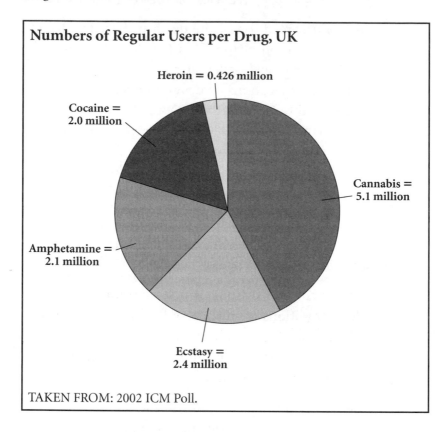

Numbers of Regular Users per Drug, UK

Heroin = 0.426 million

Cocaine = 2.0 million

Cannabis = 5.1 million

Amphetamine = 2.1 million

Ecstasy = 2.4 million

TAKEN FROM: 2002 ICM Poll.

Harm reduction principles should naturally inform policy for legal and illegal drugs. However, running harm reduction initiatives within a harm-maximising prohibitionist framework is clearly not a rational or sustainable policy. It can be very useful for dealing with some of the negative health harms of illegal drug misuse, but it has no impact on harms associated with illegal production and supply. . . .

It seems clear that the new resources for drug treatment have not arisen because of an outbreak of compassion for problematic drug users, rather a realisation that enforced abstinence amongst dependent users may reduce offending. The money now flowing into drug treatment, administered by the Home Office rather than the Department of Health, can be seen primarily as a crime reduction measure. No matter how much treatment is made available, a significant majority will continue to use and a minority of this group will offend to support their illegal habits.

We are now in a situation where the enforcement of prohibition is creating offenders then using the same criminal justice system to coerce these offenders into treatment, aimed primarily at reducing offending. It is a perverse undertaking that holds little or no hope of success.

The United States' Meth Crackdown Is Counterproductive and Displaces Production to Mexico

Kari Huus

In the following article, reporter Kari Huus brings to light problems resulting from prohibition in the United States. Meth production being displaced to Mexico is an example of the "balloon effect," a term often used in criticism of prohibition-based drug policy: as a balloon is squeezed in one place, the air moves elsewhere. As the United States has ramped up on lab raids and restriction of pseudoephedrine sales, the void is being filled elsewhere by international drug cartels. Reporter Kari Huus has been with MSNBC.com since 1996. A former Fulbright scholar, Huus was a staff writer for the Far Eastern Economic Review. *She also worked for* Newsweek, *while living in Beijing.*

As you read, consider the following questions:

1. Why, according to Huus, is it nearly impossible for law enforcement to concentrate on specific regions or countries to cut off the supply of meth?

2. What is Congress doing to combat this crisis, according to the author?

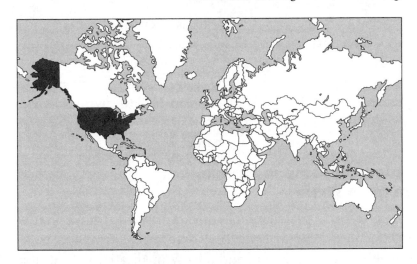

3. Which three countries are the biggest producers of ephedrine and pseudoephedrine?

After years of raiding "redneck labs" and arresting local methamphetamine cooks, drug squads in Georgia appeared to be gaining the upper hand on the makeshift operations in 2004, when the number of busts declined sharply from a peak of more than 800 the previous year.

But the glow of success quickly faded as international drug cartels distributing a purer form of the drug known as "ice" rushed in to fill the void.

"The labs start to decline and you're happy," said Phil Price, special agent in charge of regional drug enforcement for the Georgia Bureau of Investigation. "But the imported meth has really hit us hard. . . . It's cheaper now to buy it on the streets."

Price said the shift has made the drug so abundant that distributors now commonly "front" up to two pounds of ice to street dealers on credit. It also has turned the Atlanta area into a distribution hub for the East Coast, he said.

"Unfortunately, I think we're going to go through what Miami went through with cocaine," he said.

What is happening in Georgia is occurring in many other states, the unexpected result of a strong law enforcement push against home meth labs and new limits on the purchase of cold remedies used to make the drug. The state's dilemma also illustrates the difficulties of America's battle with methamphetamine, which has addictive powers comparable to crack cocaine, but is in many ways harder to control.

Ingredients Easy to Obtain, Tough to Police

The so-called "precursor chemicals" used to make meth— pseudoephedrine and ephedrine—are inexpensive and widely available in common cold and allergy medications. That ubiquity makes it impossible for law enforcement to concentrate on specific regions or countries in an effort to choke off the supply.

"Unlike drugs derived from organic materials, such as cocaine or heroin, (methamphetamine) production is not limited to a specific geographic region," Anne Patterson, assistant secretary of the State Department's Bureau for International Narcotics and Law Enforcement Affairs, testified before the Senate Foreign Affairs Committee in June [2006].

Its effects also ensure a steady demand.

Once inhaled, injected or smoked, meth creates euphoria and energy that can last for several days. But the frenzied flights are followed by depression and exhaustion that drive the need for the next fix. Eventually, the relentless pursuit of meth drives many users out of their middle- and upper-class lives into a grim existence of crime, poverty and deteriorating health on the streets.

Crackdown on Medication Purchases

Alarmed by the spread of the drug across the United States from its initial foothold on the West Coast, many communities have passed ordinances to made it harder for home cooks to buy large quantities of cold and allergy medications.

Congress entered the fray by passing the Combat Methamphetamine Epidemic Act in March [2006] as part of the renewal of the anti-terror Patriot Act, placing restrictions on retail pseudoephedrine purchases across the nation.

The federal government also has stepped up support on the front lines, funding training for local law enforcement agencies to help them find and safely dismantle the highly toxic meth labs.

As a result, lab seizures nationwide peaked in 2003 at more than 17,000 and have declined by nearly a third, to around 12,000 in 2005, according to the U.S. Drug Enforcement Administration [DEA].

"Most of the meth smuggled into the United States is produced in Mexico, using chemicals diverted by the ton from pharmaceutical companies in Asia."

But the battle gets tougher as it shifts to the global theater.

Helping Police Global Trade

At the moment, federal drug enforcement officials say most of the meth smuggled into the United States is produced in Mexico, using chemicals diverted by the ton from pharmaceutical companies in Asia. But as the global spread of the drug illustrates, there are many routes to market.

Recognizing the new international threat, Washington is taking legislative and diplomatic initiatives to ensure cooperation from the global players in the meth trade—manufacturing centers like Mexico and the world's biggest producers of pseudoephedrine and ephedrine, China, India and Germany.

At the United Nations, the United States pushed through a resolution that calls on countries to submit a yearly estimate of their legitimate need for the chemicals and to provide information on all exports—both bulk shipments and those of pharmaceutical preparations. Previously, those ingredients were uncontrolled, a gaping loophole in regulations that allowed millions of tablets containing pseudoephedrine and ephedrine to be sold on the black market.

Under the Combat Methamphetamine Act, the State Department also is required to certify that the biggest exporters and importers of the chemicals cooperate with the United States, with the threat of withdrawal of foreign aid hanging over those that do not.

The U.S. initiative is working to a degree. The DEA says the United States has seen increasing cooperation from Mexico, China, India, and Germany in sharing intelligence and conducting joint enforcement operations. The urgency of the mission is clear because they too are witnessing a rising tide of meth abuse, the DEA says.

But political will doesn't always translate into control over agile drug trafficking organizations.

"We're seeing ephedrine shipped from India and China to South Africa and then from there to South and Central America," DEA administrator Karen Tandy said in a recent speech in Canada. "Chinese ephedrine is being diverted through Cairo on its way to Mexico. And ephedrine and pseudoephedrine are being diverted in other African countries, including Angola, the Democratic Republic of Congo, Kenya, and Mozambique."

Mexican authorities say that despite such criminal resourcefulness, limits imposed in 2004 on imports of pseudoephedrine and ephedrine and restrictions on the ports that shippers can use are paying off. The Federal Commission for Health Concerns told NBC this month [September 2006] that legal imports of pseudoephedrine have been more than halved, with 72 tons imported in the first nine months of 2006, compared to a total of 216 tons in 2004.

Mexico also has strengthened security for movement and storage of these chemicals, though the precautions aren't always sufficient to stop determined criminals.

In late July [2006], gunmen raided a pharmaceutical company in Mexico City, killing four guards and stealing about 2,200 pounds of pseudoephedrine.

"In a 2005 crackdown on the meth trade, China says it seized more than 130 tons of smuggled pseudoephedrine in nine months."

Within weeks, the Mexican authorities seized about 220 pounds of finished meth at a "super lab" near Guadalajara. Mexican officials later said the chemicals used to make it had been imported legally from China, but did not explain how they were obtained by the meth producers.

Beijing Battles Local Interests

China also is cracking down on the diversion of the chemicals from its massive pharmaceutical industry by beefing up security and regulations on pseudoephedrine producers, in part because domestic use of synthetic drugs, including methamphetamine and ecstasy, is climbing.

In a marked change, U.S. officials say Beijing has started conducting joint investigations with U.S. drug agents and sharing trafficking intelligence. In a 2005 crackdown on the meth trade, China says it seized more than 130 tons of smuggled pseudoephedrine in nine months.

But chaos and corruption at the local level frequently undermine Beijing's regulations and policies.

A news report in June [2006] gave a glimpse of what Beijing is up against: Hong Kong's *South China Morning Post* said government drug agents arrested 100 police officers in Shenyang for protecting a local meth smuggler.

Reports like that suggests the government's crackdown will have a limited impact, said David Bachman, a professor of Chinese affairs in the Jackson School of International Studies at the University of Washington.

Methamphetamine Supply

The most urgent priority of the federal government toward reducing the supply of methamphetamine in the United States will be to tighten the international market for chemical precursors, such as pseudoephedrine and ephedrine, used to produce the drug. Most of the methamphetamine used in America—probably between 75 and 85 percent—is made with chemical precursors that are diverted at some point from the international stream of commerce. The remainder of the methamphetamine is produced from chemical precursors that are purchased at the wholesale or retail level and diverted for use in illicit production in the United States. Although domestic enforcement continues to be a priority, the impact of state laws controlling retail access to precursors, together with federal, state, and local enforcement efforts, has had a significant impact on the domestic production of methamphetamine. As a result, a larger proportion of methamphetamine consumed in the United States is now coming across the border as a final product, compared to that which is produced domestically in small, toxic laboratories (STLs).

Executive Office of the President of the United States,
Synthetic Drug Control Strategy: A Focus on
Methamphetamine and Prescription Drug Abuse, *2006.*

"It is the type of problem as in software piracy . . . where there are strong incentives not to comply . . . (including) profits, jobs," he said. "We've seen the stink the U.S. can make on (intellectual property rights), and how little progress has been made."

The challenges of the global meth trade help explain why local officials in the United States still consider meth to be their biggest problem, according to a recent survey by the National Association of Counties.

That certainly holds true in the greater Atlanta area, where officials are seeing clear evidence of the involvement of the Mexican gangs in the meth trade.

On August 16 [2006], officers seized a U.S.-record 174 pounds of the drug in Buford, Ga., about 30 miles northeast of Atlanta. The mark didn't last long, as a week later police in nearby Gainesville arrested dealers with 341 pounds of ice—a stash worth an estimated $50 million on the street.

From Mexican 'Super Labs' to U.S. Streets

Authorities said organized gangs had smuggled the drug into the United States from Mexico, where it was probably manufactured at "super labs."

Farther to the north, Sheriff Steve Wilson of Walker County, Ga., isn't contemplating laying off any jailers even though his jurisdiction on Georgia's northern border with Tennessee is currently experiencing a breather in the meth epidemic.

At the height of what he calls the war against "redneck labs" making meth, Wilson said his jail—capacity 210—was jammed with 230 inmates, most of them in for meth production and related crimes.

But even though the inmate population is down to 150, Wilson is bracing for the next wave of meth crime, convinced that the Mexican gangs that are plaguing counties to the south are even now reversing Sherman's march on Atlanta during the Civil War.

"What we believe is going to happen is that we've become so strict on the purchase of pseudoephedrine ... that we will see a lot more Mexican meth," he said. "They'll make it by hundreds of pounds. I know it's coming."

Periodical Bibliography

The following articles have been selected to supplement the diverse views presented in this chapter.

Abigail Curtis — "US Democrats Call Colombia Drug Eradication Failure, Demand Aid Cuts," The Associated Press, *International Herald Tribune*, June 6, 2007.

Paul Fishstein — "Poppy Paradox in Afghanistan," *Boston Globe*, September 16, 2007. www.boston.com.

Frontline — "The Meth Epidemic: Mexican Meth," interview by Steve Suo, PBS, WGBH, 2006. www.pbs.org.

Jens Erik Gould — "U.S. Effort to Kill Coca Failing in Colombia," *San Francisco Chronicle*, March 11, 2007. www.sfgate.com/chronicle.

Peter van Ham and Jorrit Kamminga — "Poppies for Peace: Reforming Afghanistan's Opium Industry," *The Washington Quarterly*, vol. 30, no. 1, 2006–2007, pp. 69–81.

Ali A. Jalali, Robert B. Oakley et al. — "Combating Opium in Afghanistan," *Strategic Forum*, no. 224, 2006.

Joseph Kirschke — "Despite Little Success in Colombia, Some U.S. Officials Continue to Push Crop Spraying in Afghanistan," *World Politics Review*, February 8, 2008. www.worldpoliticsreview.com.

Donald G. McNeil Jr. — "Opium in Afghanistan: Eradicate or Subsidize?" *International Herald Tribune*, October 14, 2007.

Anthony Papa — "It's Time to Rethink Drug Prohibition," Counterpunch, March 15, 2007. www.counterpunch.org.

Transnational Institute — "Colombia Coca Cultivation Survey Results: A Question of Methods," *Drug Policy Briefing No. 22*, June 2007. www.tni.org.

GLOBAL VIEWPOINTS

CHAPTER 3

Environmental Degradation Due to Drugs and Eradication Methods

The Production of Drugs Is Causing Global Environmental Damage

United States Drug Enforcement Administration (DEA)

The following viewpoint investigates how drug production is progressively damaging the environment. Trees are being destroyed as more and more room is cleared out for illicit drug crops, while pesticides and herbicides are being applied carelessly—harming valuable land. Consequently, deforestation has become a problem on a global scale. Contamination of the water supply has also become a serious threat as hazardous drug by-products are being dumped into rivers and streams. It is becoming increasingly clear that drug production is taking its toll on the environment. The Just Think Twice Web site was created as a resource for teens by the Drug Enforcement Administration (DEA), the United States' government agency enforcing the laws and regulations relating to the production and distribution of controlled substances in the United States.

As you read, consider the following questions:

1. As explained in the following viewpoint, how might the burning of rain forests to create land for illegal drug farming contribute to global climate change?

2. How are insurgent groups involved in the drug trade causing significant environmental damage in Colombia?

United States Drug Enforcement Administration (DEA), "Costs to Society: Damage to Environment," *DEA-Demand Reduction*. www.justthinktwice.com. Copyright © 2006 DEA.

3. As cited in the article, for every pound of methamphetamine produced, how many pounds of toxic waste are generated?

One of the most often overlooked and ignored aspects of the illegal drug trade is the cost of drug production to the environment. From the clear-cutting [removal of trees to make room for crops] of rain forests in Central and South America for the planting of coca fields, to the destruction of national forests in the United States for the growing of marijuana, to the dumping of hazardous waste by-products into the water table after the manufacture of methamphetamine, illegal drugs have a far-reaching impact on the environment. These activities have consequences for the health of the groundwater, streams, rivers, wildlife, pets, and the farmers living in those areas. Illegal drug production contributes to deforestation, reduced biodiversity, and increased erosion, and contributes to air pollution and global climate change.

It's not a problem we can ignore, and it's our problem too. We're outraged when oil-tankers spill fuel into our waters, yet every day meth cookers poison our buildings, soil and water supplies—who's concerned about protecting those environments? We're paying the environmental costs—all of us.

Damage to the Rain Forest

Rain forests cover only 6 percent of the earth's surface, yet account for more than 50 percent of the earth's plant species. Burning of rain forests for illegal drug farmland releases greenhouse gases. The increase in these emissions is being studied as a possible contributor to global climate change.

Coca and opium production and cocaine manufacturing have a tremendous impact on the environment of South America. One quarter (25 percent) of all of the deforestation that has taken place in Peru in modern times is associated with clear-cutting and burning to prepare land for the planting of coca bushes. Over the past twenty years, 2.4 million hectares of rain forest (1 hectare equals 10,000 square meters or 2.47 acres)—an area roughly the size of El Salvador—has been lost to drug production fields in the Andean region of Peru, Bolivia and Colombia. One hectare of coca field requires four hectares of forest to be cleared.

As a result of cocaine production, 14,800 tons of dangerous chemicals are discharged into the Amazon River basin each year.

Burning and cutting down rain forests to make room for drug fields exposes the thin layers of topsoil to accelerated erosion. Nearby streams and rivers are more susceptible to increased and prolonged flooding. In the late 1970s, the Huallaga River in Peru experienced significant flooding, resulting from increased runoff from coca fields cleared out of the surrounding jungle. Plots of land for coca crops are typically useful for growing for four to ten years. At the end of that time, the coca farmers move to a new area and cut or burn down more jungle to start new fields for coca cultivation.

Chemicals like ethyl ether, acetone, ammonia, sulfuric acid and hydrochloric acid are used in jungle laboratories to turn coca leaves into coca paste and finally cocaine. 14,800 tons of these chemicals are discharged into the Amazon River basin each year in the production of cocaine. The chemicals discharged from jungle drug laboratories, combined with the agricultural imbalance of coca growing fields, endanger 210 mammal species, 600 bird species, 170 reptile species, 100 amphibian species and 600 fish species in the Amazon and Orinoco River systems alone.

Additionally, terrorist and insurgency groups in Colombia, with links to the drug trade, regularly bomb pipelines in that country in an effort to overthrow the government and terrorize the population. These pipeline bombings result in signifi-

---

Devastating Consequences

The United States consumes nearly 260 metric tons of cocaine every year, which is grown and processed in the fragile environments of South America. The result has been the destruction of almost 6 million acres of fragile tropical forest. . . .

The rapidly eroding rain forests may mean that scientists may not find potential cures for deadly diseases (one in six prescription drugs has a tropical source). The loss of rain forests also contributes to changes in the global climate. Pollution of waterways will perhaps permanently eradicate species of plants and animals, in addition to releasing carcinogens into drinking water for generations to come.

U.S. Department of State,
"U.S. Links Illegal Drug Production, Environmental Damage,"
Office of National Drug Control Policy Press Release,
April 18, 2003. http://USinfo.state.gov.

---

cant oil spills with environmental damage. The damage is not only related to cocaine production; opium (for heroin) production has also resulted in deforestation. Each hectare of productive opium field requires the clearing of approximately two and a half hectares of forest. 120 to 230 tons of soil per hectare is lost to erosion.

Drugs and Environmental Damage in the United States

It's happening in our own backyard. Meth labs, marijuana plots, urban streets littered with syringes and vials. Our fragile environment is being damaged by drug traffickers.

The production of methamphetamine has skyrocketed in the United States since the early 1990s. The chemicals used in the making of the drug include lye, red phosphorus, hydriodic acid, and iodine. One pound of finished methamphetamine results in five to six pounds of hazardous waste by-products. These chemicals are often dumped into the ground near a laboratory, contaminating the local water.

The chemicals used in methamphetamine laboratories and the finished product are very toxic. Children who live in houses with such laboratories often test positive for the drug. The cleanup of a laboratory is time consuming, dangerous, and expensive. The cost runs from five hundred dollars and a few hours of work to tens of thousands of dollars and weeks or months of work. Every year houses and motel rooms are torn down due to their extensive contamination by toxic methamphetamine laboratory chemicals.

For every pound of methamphetamine produced, between five and six pounds of highly toxic waste is generated. Remote areas offer easy disposal of toxic by-products of the manufacturing process. It can take up to three or more days and more than $100,000 to clean up contaminated soil, destroy buildings, and remove toxic chemicals from drug sites.

More than 2,500,000 marijuana plants have been found and destroyed in national forests in the United States since 1997. These marijuana farms have been planted in protected areas, often destroying the surrounding areas by the careless use of herbicides and pesticides.

American Meth Labs Pose a Hazardous Threat to the Environment

Ben Arnoldy

Many opponents of the war on drugs argue that the prohibition and eradication of drug crops like opium and cocaine have perpetuated the demand for synthetic drugs in the United States. It is now estimated that over a million methamphetamine (meth) labs exist in the country, with drugmakers cooking up this drug in kitchens using dangerous household chemicals. In the following article, Ben Arnoldy investigates how homes, apartments, and even hotel rooms, used as meth labs have become hazardous toxic waste sites. Various states, now faced with significant environmental and health concerns, must address the risks and begin to establish laws for property cleanup and disclosure. Ben Arnoldy is a staff writer for The Christian Science Monitor.

As you read, consider the following questions:

1. According to the following viewpoint, approximately how many meth labs have been reported to the Drug Enforcement Administration since 1998?

2. As cited in the article, how many states require property sellers to disclose former meth labs?

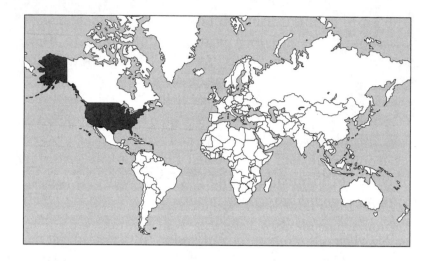

3. When does the Environmental Protection Agency expect it will be able to offer standards demonstrating health risks associated with meth lab exposure?

Hotel rooms, apartment complexes, and homes aren't your typical toxic waste sites. But then, methamphetamine isn't your typical drug.

The drug—which makers often cook up in their kitchens using household chemicals and tools—is potent enough to transform homes into hazmat zones. When law officers bust a meth lab, the drug-making materials are carted away. But what happens next to such former sites—numbering more than 100,000 across the country—varies dramatically.

States Face Environmental Threats

Some states, led by Colorado, have enacted tough regulations that require former lab sites to undergo a formal safety assessment—and more cleanup, if needed—before they can be rehabited. The laws are prompted by the extreme toxicity of the chemicals used to cook meth, and suspicions about the long-term effects of chemical remnants in the air and on surfaces. Other states mandate home sellers to disclose the presence of former meth labs.

The patchwork of state approaches reflects the uneven spread of the drug, the potential costs of cleanup, and concerns about setting safety standards in the absence of definitive scientific research, experts say.

"Until we fully understand what the potential health effects can be, we feel that it's better that states are more proactive as opposed to reactive," says Shawn Arbuckle with the National Jewish Medical and Research Center in Denver. Better safe than sorry, he adds.

Cooking meth just once contaminates a building with traces of acids and iodine in the air, as well as large amounts of meth on surfaces ranging from sofas to ventilation ducts, according to research done at National Jewish. Hydrochloric acid is an irritant to the eyes, skin, and respiratory tract, and iodine can trigger asthmatic reactions, says Mr. Arbuckle.

Business contractors have sprung up to assess and decontaminate former meth labs. Basic cleanup involves hauling away carpets, furniture, drapes, and other items that can absorb airborne particles. Then all surfaces are thoroughly cleaned, including ceilings and walls. Sometimes dry wall must be replaced.

Less than one percent of the approximately 1.5 million meth labs operating in the United States have been decontaminated.

Meth Lab Cleanup Co., based in Idaho, charges about $300 to $500 for a consultation, assessment, and site sampling. Basic decontamination costs from $4,000 to $6,000 for a modest home. But expenses can quickly skyrocket when further work is required.

Joseph Mazzuca, the company's operation director, says cooks sometimes disconnect stove vents to prevent neighbors from smelling suspicious fumes. Instead, the vent pipe is stuffed into the insulation, creating a bigger mess. He's also had to move a home to remove topsoil contaminated by dumped chemicals. While he has yet to see a well contaminated by dumping, he has seen PVC piping melted away.

Three-quarters of his calls are to sites that never involved law enforcement, suggesting there are many labs beyond the 100,000 reported to the Drug Enforcement Administration [DEA] since 1998.

"Our estimate is that there are about a million and a half meth labs in America, and less than 1 percent of them have been decontaminated," he says.

Cleanup and Disclosure Guidelines Are Inconsistent

He's noticed other disturbing trends. He sees children's clothing or toys at most sites. And 75 percent of labs are rentals. "Typically landlords, especially on the bad side of town, don't worry about [cleanup] so much unless there's a law," he says.

Increasingly, states are addressing that, particularly those that have dealt with the problem the longest, such as in the Midwest and West. Colorado has been at the forefront, forcing property owners not only to have the mess cleaned up, but to adhere to a very specific set of procedures and testing requirements.

Northeastern states—which have yet to see high numbers of home labs—have been slower to adopt new laws.

Connecticut released a new set of nonbinding guidelines following a bust last year [2005] of two labs in East Hampton. After federal authorities came and went, the landlord of one of the properties, a small ranch house on a wooded road, began his own cleanup. He then sold the home, according to a local public health official and a former resident, without notifying the health department or telling the buyer beforehand of the existence of the former lab. (The attorney involved in the sale declined to comment, and neither the current owner nor the selling landowner could be reached.)

Hawaii Tests Cleanup Law

When Maui vice officers raided a clandestine methamphetamine lab in a Wailuku apartment last year, among those notified was a state office responsible for overseeing decontamination of such hazardous sites.

About thirty days and $12,000 later, the cleanup was completed, said Anna Fernandez, meth lab cleanup project coordinator for the state Department of Health's Hazard Evaluation and Emergency Response Office.

The landlord later received a Department of Health certificate saying the rental was safe to be occupied again.

Fernandez said the incident was the first—and so far only—test of a state law enacted in 2006 to establish guidelines for the decontamination of illegal methamphetamine manufacturing sites.

The law has generated interest from residents, including some landlords and rental property managers.

Lila Fujimoto,
"Drug Operations Can Leave Toxic Hazards Behind,"
Maui News, *March 25, 2008.*

Connecticut still does not compel an owner to decontaminate except in serious cases, and property sellers still are not required to disclose former meth labs—a requirement now in fourteen states.

"There is not uniformity across all of the states, and frequently, people look to the federal government to step in at that point [to put] out something that can serve as a standard for all states to at least consider," says Kevin Teichman, a scientist with the Environmental Protection Agency [EPA].

The EPA aims to offer standards by 2011 tied to demonstrated health risks. Arbuckle says that determining what is a healthy level of exposure over a long period of time will require more research—something Mr. Teichman says the agency is pushing.

Federal money is also going to assessments and cleanups. The EPA has revised its definition of brownfields [industrial or commercial property that is abandoned and often has environmental contamination] to include former meth labs, though grants can go only to groups such as nonprofit organizations, not homeowners. The DEA offers free training and equipment to first responders and shoulders much of the bill for a contractor to remove lab materials whenever called to a scene.

"Technically the contractor has cleaned it out," says Steve Robertson, a special agent assigned to DEA headquarters. "If it was my property, I would rip out the carpet, I would scrub the floors, I would repaint everything, because these . . . are very hazardous chemicals."

Yemen's Addiction to Qat Is Exhausting Its Water Supply

Jonathon Walz

In the following viewpoint, Jonathon Walz raises awareness about a less familiar drug known as "qat"—a narcotic shrub with euphoric properties. In the Arabian country of Yemen, qat is a significant part of the culture. Widely consumed, qat is an important cash crop and provides a source of employment for a large number of Yemenis. In a country already suffering from a shortage of renewable water resources, however, its cultivation is leading to an environmental crisis. Walz is a graduate of the University of South Dakota and a two-time recipient of the David L. Boren National Security Education Program Scholarship. In 2007, he was awarded a U.S. Department of State Critical Language Scholarship to study in Yemen.

As you read, consider the following questions:

1. What percentage of personal income can be accounted to expenditures on qat in Yemen?

2. According to Walz, how is Yemen attempting to meet its increasing water needs?

3. As indicated in the following viewpoint, what challenges have the Yemeni government and agricultural nongovernmental organizations (NGOs) faced in encouraging alternative cash crops?

Jonathon Walz, "Yemen, Drugs and the Water Table," *The Globalist*, November 12, 2007. Reproduced by permission.-

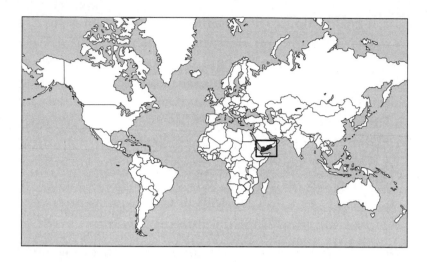

Yemen is home to a unique landscape that boasts a moderate climate, fertile valleys, towering mountains and a culture that is nothing if not unique. So attractive is Yemen that, upon its discovery by the Romans, it was given the name Arabia Felix—the "blessed Arabia."

Over the past two millennia, Yemen has developed a less positive reputation amongst foreigners. Today [2007] Westerners are more likely to identify Yemen with the 2000 bombing of the *U.S.S. Cole* or as the ancestral homeland of Osama bin Laden—rather than recognizing its unique culture and landscape.

No Shortage of Problems

As the country attempts to reinvent itself as a pro-Western ally in the so-called war on terrorism, it faces a number of difficulties. With a poor economy that is often cited as a case study for the failures of IMF [International Monetary Fund] structural adjustment programs, declining oil output, one of the world's highest population growth rates, and a mounting battle with Islamic extremism, Yemen's government is not short on problems.

In the decades since Yemen's independence, the country has also seen a dramatic rise in its consumption of a drug called qat.

The substance, which is also known by its Latin name *Catha edulis*, is a narcotic shrub that elicits feelings of euphoria when its leaves are chewed. Qat consumption is so prevalent in Yemen that its use has become nearly synonymous with Yemeni culture.

The consumption of qat in Yemen has parallels with the traditional use of coca leaves in South America—and has been widely criticized by foreign governments and NGOs [nongovernmental organizations] because of its negative impacts on Yemeni society and its potential for becoming a popular drug in Europe and North America.

Regardless of one's views on the country's use of qat, it is exceedingly clear that there are mounting costs for Yemen's consumption of the substance.

Economic and Environmental Costs

Recent research by the World Bank has found that personal expenditures on qat in the country account for about 10 percent of personal income.

In Yemen, up to 25 percent of usable working hours are devoted to chewing qat.

Given that the substance is consumed by all segments of society, qat expenditures as a percentage of family income tend to be highest among Yemen's poor.

In addition to the financial costs of chewing, a recent World Bank report notes that the practice of consuming the substance during afternoon hours has inhibited the development of a productive workforce in Yemen—with up to 25 percent of usable working hours being devoted to chewing.

Although Yemenis are currently paying the economic price for their consumption of qat, an environmental crisis may be the drug's enduring legacy. Yemen naturally suffers from a shortage of renewable water resources.

If Yemen's renewable water resources were apportioned on a per capita basis, each citizen would be entitled to around 220 cubic meters of water annually. This is distressing when compared with average consumption rates in the Middle East and globally—at 1,250 and 7,500 cubic meters per year, respectively.

Exacerbating the Water Crisis

This lack of water has resulted in the mining of non-rechargeable aquifers [underground beds of earth or rock] in order to meet the country's increasing water needs.

The country's infatuation with qat is playing a major role in the water crisis because of the amount of water needed to cultivate the crop. As production increases to match the rising demand for the substance, water becomes scarcer.

It is estimated that the amount of land used to cultivate qat has increased thirteen-fold in the past three decades.

Today, a third of all groundwater extraction in Yemen is used for the cultivation of qat. Not only are Yemenis robbing future generations of water through their consumption of nonrenewable fossil aquifers, the effects of overuse are being seen today. The water table is falling by between two and six meters per year in parts of the country.

A number of experts have claimed that Sana'a [Yemen's capital] will be the first of the world's capitals to exhaust its water resources—possibly before the end of the decade. As can be expected, qat is a major contributor to this shortage. In the early 1990s, it was determined that the amount of water used to cultivate qat in the city and its surrounding areas accounted for twice what was being used for human consumption.

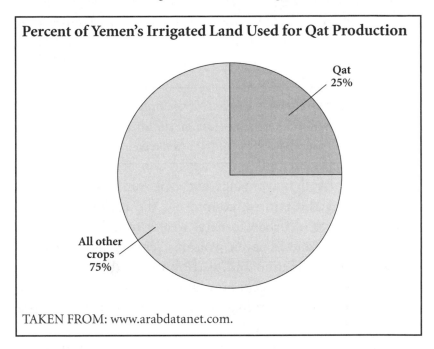

Percent of Yemen's Irrigated Land Used for Qat Production

Qat
25%

All other
crops
75%

TAKEN FROM: www.arabdatanet.com.

While Sana'a's water crisis is troubling, other parts of the country suffer from similar—if not more severe—water shortages.

In a number of villages, fits of violence have broken out over the scarce water resources. Most notably, a 1999 conflict over a spring near the city of Ta'iz left six dead and sixty injured.

Although there has been discussion in Yemen's NGO community about conflict mediation tactics that can limit such conflicts, there is clearly a need to address the underlying problem. Unfortunately, there are no easy ways to wean Yemen off qat.

The Drug's Economic Importance

With 73 percent of Yemen's population living in rural areas, it is not surprising that agriculture is a staple of the country's economy. For Yemen's farmers, qat is their primary cash crop.

Although qat accounts for just 10 percent of cultivated land, it constitutes a third of the country's agricultural GDP [gross domestic product]—and 6 percent of total GDP.

One in seven working Yemenis are employed directly in the production and distribution of the drug qat; for Yemen farmers, it is their primary cash crop.

In a country that competes with the Sudan for bragging rights in being the poorest country in the region, qat is an important source of urban-to-rural wealth transfer.

Additionally, one in seven working Yemenis are employed directly in the production and distribution of the drug. Given qat's importance to the economy, any attempt to curb its use must also provide an alternative source of income for those disadvantaged by the shift.

This task has proved difficult for the Yemeni government and agricultural NGOs. Cash crops that have been suggested as alternatives to qat either require additional water to produce or give an inferior return on labor. A recent study has suggested that qat is ten to twenty times more profitable than competing crops.

Yemen's dependence on qat has created quite the conundrum for its political leaders. The economic costs of limiting production may make any plan politically infeasible. At the same time, the environmental implications suggest that they can't afford not to change.

Only time will tell how the problem ends. Unfortunately, time—like water—is not Yemen's abundant resource.

Colombia's Legal Crops and Forests Are Wrongly Destroyed by Eradication

Bill Weinberg

In the following viewpoint, Bill Weinberg's journey into Colombia's Cimitarra Valley provides an unsettling account of damage resulting from U.S.-funded fumigation flights. Weinberg argues that residents are experiencing a host of ailments after being exposed to aerial spraying of glyphosate; in addition, food crops have been carelessly eradicated along with coca bushes and land has been destroyed and rendered useless for farming. Weinberg is an award-winning journalist and editor of World War 4 Report *(www.ww4report.com). He is currently writing on a book about the failures of Plan Colombia.*

As you read, consider the following questions:

1. As explained in the following viewpoint, why is it difficult for the campesinos to make money selling their legal crops?

2. Besides poisoning crops, how is the aerial spraying damaging the land?

3. Why, according to the following viewpoint, is the African palm a poor alternative crop to coca?

Bill Weinberg, "Between Dyncorp and the A.U.C: Glyphosate and Paramilitary Terror in Colombia's Cimitarra Valley," *World War 4 Report*, August 27, 2003. www.ww4report .com. Reproduced by permission.

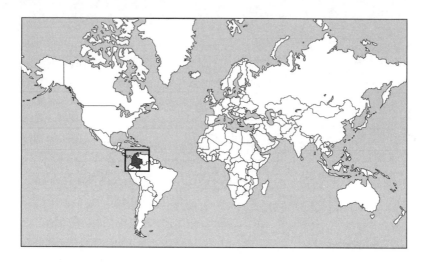

Leaving Barrancabermeja [northeastern Colombian city] in a canoa—a small launch with an outboard motor—the perilous patchwork of armed groups that vie for control of Colombia's Medio Magdalena region becomes immediately obvious. Navy gunboats painted in camo line the shore along the huge oil refinery that looms over the Rio Magdalena. Just a few minutes later, a little past the edge of the city, paramilitary checkpoints on either bank survey the river traffic. They don't stop our boat because we are flying the flag of Peace Brigades International from the bow, and the paras [paramilitaries] like to give foreign human rights observers a wide berth. There are practically no suburbs—just past the para checkpoint we find ourselves in an endless expanse of wetlands and jungle broken only by the most primitive of campesino [farmer, peasant] settlements. Herons laze on the green banks as we make our way north to the Rio Cimitarra—a tributary of the Magdalena where coca growers, paras and guerillas have all staked their turf.

I've come to this remote and conflicted region with a commission from the Colombian rights group Humanidades Vigentes, accompanied by two representatives of the Peace Brigades for our protection. We spend a mosquito-haunted night at Puerto Machete, the little riverside settlement where the canoa drops us off. Then it is a four-hour hike along an unimproved dirt road and jungle trails to our destination: the little campesino vereda (settlement) of La Floresta. The last hour on the trail seems endless. We wade streams, sink knee-deep into mud, crawl under barbed-wire fences, climb and descend hill after hill. When a campesino from La Floresta passes us on his mule, I ask hopefully "Falta mucho?" (Is it much further?) He nods gravely and answers "Si, siempre." Yes, always.

Poison from the Skies, Fear on the Land

There is no electricity in La Floresta, and no running water. The only sign of any government presence is in the form of destroyed land.

Our commission has come to document the impact of aerial glyphosate fumigation of the settlement's lands to wipe out coca crops. The impacts are obvious as soon as we arrive. Marina Salguero, the official health promoter for Floresta and nearby settlements, who is licensed by the local municipal government of Cantagallo, maintains an extremely makeshift clinic in a little hilltop hut. A thin old man with a big rash on his leg sits in the hut with a penicillin IV in his arm. His skin irritation, a result of being caught in his fields when the fumigation overflight swooped down, has become infected, Salguero says.

"I get cases like this all the time," she says. "Children with head pain, vomiting, diarrhea, skin irritation. Every time the planes come." She points out a stretch of land on a nearby hill glaringly brown and dead in the green landscape—the result of the last fumigation, fifteen days earlier. The brown stretch is right beside a house. "Their home, their kitchen was fumigated. Their crops are destroyed—maize, platano, yucca."

Salguero admits that coca is grown at La Floresta—"just to have a little money," she says. "You saw how bad the road is here." She notes that having to haul out legal crops on the road—followed by a river trip to the nearest town, with paras sometimes stealing whatever goods the campesinos carry— means the cost of getting crops to market eats virtually all profits. In contrast, men come to the vereda to buy the coca and carry it out themselves.

"When the campesinos take us on a tour . . . they all tell [the] same story—legal food crops and forest [were] destroyed along with the coca bushes."

"We are completely abandoned by the government here— municipal, departmental, national," Salguero protests. "What alternative do we have? I'm responsible for three veredas, and I don't even have a thermometer."

Legal Crops Unjustly Destroyed

On this recently settled agricultural frontier, where land is cleared from the rain forest with no oversight, the campesinos have no ability to interact with the bureaucracy for credit or aid. "Here the land is not titled," says Salguero. "Everyone has his predio (plot) and works it."

When the campesinos take us on a tour of the vereda, showing us the plots which have been destroyed by fumigation flights, they all tell [the] same story—legal food crops and forest [were] destroyed along with the coca bushes. They pull up the dead stalks of yucca, killed before they could be harvested. They claim over 100 chickens have been killed by glyphosate spraying in the village since the first fumigation flights in 2001. Sometimes it is clear that the legal crops were destroyed because they were planted amid coca crops. Sometimes it looks as if the glyphosate drifted, or was sprayed wildly wide of its target. Everywhere it is clear that the spraying is degrading these hard-won lands not only by direct poisoning, but by destroying the plant cover that holds down the soil, leading to erosion and muddy streams.

"As long as fumigation continues, no alternative crop program will make much difference."

The fumigation flights, carried out by planes from the private firm Dyncorp under contract to the U.S. State Department, are accompanied by up to seven helicopters from the Colombian Army or National Police. They take off from the airport in Barrancabermeja. Army ground troops also come to burn down coca paste labs from time to time, or to search for guerillas. The campesinos complain that the troops demand mules for transport and chickens for food without compensation.

Laboratory of the Counter-Reform

The Medio Magdalena region, which includes the Cimitarra Valley and straddles the [political] departments of Antioquia, Santander, Cesar and Bolivar, has ironically been dubbed by the Colombian government and foreign aid agencies a "Laboratory of Peace." The program includes a European Union-backed proposal to promote African palm oil as an alternative crop and a spur to economic development in the region. [Secretary of the Cimitarra Valley Campesino Association's Governing Committee Miguel] Cifuentes opposes the African palm proposal as a technocratic pseudo-solution. "It is a monoculture, [the use of land for growing only one kind of crop] and it displaces traditional crops, worsening the food crisis in region and increasing campesino debt," he says.

Jorge Enrique Gomez is Medio Magdalena regional chief of the Defensoria del Pueblo, an official human rights watchdog created by Colombia's 1991 constitutional reform. He has been at his post since February 2002, when he returned to the Medio Magdalena after ten years in exile in El Salvador and

When the Poison Fell

'We were sitting chatting outside our home when two small planes flew over very low. We went down to our fields to see what was happening. My husband said, "Look, they're dropping poison on our land." It went all over the food crops—the cassava, banana, beans, rice—and the pasture. We lost everything. And the poison went on us too. I had no coat on, so it went all over my arms. It was like cooking oil. Sticky, just like oil. I washed it off as soon as I could, but even so it made my skin itch. For several days, we all felt ill. We had fevers and eye infections. My youngest child hasn't been well since.'

This is Graciela, a 36-year-old peasant woman living in the province of Putumayo in the south of Colombia. For five years now, U.S. planes have been spraying a powerful chemical defoliant on peasant holdings as part of Plan Colombia, the U.S.-inspired—and U.S.-funded—plan to eradicate coca, the raw material from which cocaine is extracted. Thousands of peasant families have been going to local hospitals to complain of eye infections, diarrhoea, vomiting and other illnesses. It is tragically reminiscent of the Vietnam War when U.S. pilots doused land controlled by the Vietcong with a powerful defoliant, known as Agent Orange, to destroy 'cover for enemy forces'.

Sue Branford and Hugh O'Shaughnessy,
"Colombia's Killing Fields—The First Bio-War of the 21st Century,"
The Ecologist, *January 3, 2006.*

Guatemala. He fled Colombia after receiving death threats for his work documenting local human rights abuses with CREDHOS, the Barrancabermeja-based nongovernmental watchdog. Gomez believes that as long as fumigation continues, no alternative crop program will make much difference.

"To fumigate licit crops is a bad investment and a mixed message to the campesinos," he says. "Cultivation of illicit crops is a result of the lack of any government presence in the zone. Fumigations affect the poorest sector of the populace." He argues that the fumigations are not only counter-productive, but illegal.

Ecuadorians Are Suffering DNA Damage from Aerial Spray Eradication

Stephen Leahy

In the following viewpoint, Stephen Leahy explores how aerial spraying in Colombia near the Ecuador border has resulted in serious health problems for local residents. New evidence now suggests that fumigation flights dropping the chemical glyphosate have caused not only short-term illnesses, but also extensive DNA damage, which could lead to cancer and reproductive problems. Leahy is an environmental journalist who has written for dozens of international publications. He is currently the science and environment correspondent for Inter Press Service News Agency (IPS), *a wire service in Rome covering global issues, and its Latin American affiliate,* Tierramérica, *in Mexico City.*

As you read, consider the following questions:

1. Following aerial spraying, what kinds of symptoms did Ecuadorians report having experienced?
2. How might Roundup be linked to birth-related complications, as explained in the article?

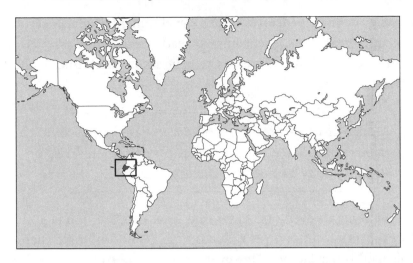

3. What findings prompted the United States Congress to obtain guarantees in 2006 preventing wetlands from being sprayed in Colombia?

Blood samples from twenty-four Ecuadorians living within three kilometers [km] of the northern border had 600 to 800 percent more damage to their chromosomes than people living eighty km away, found scientists from the Pontificia Catholic University in Quito, Ecuador.

The border residents who were tested had been exposed to the common herbicide glyphosate—sold by the U.S. agribusiness giant Monsanto under the brand Roundup—during a series of aerial sprayings by the Colombian government begun in 2000, part of the anti-drugs and counter-insurgency Plan Colombia, financed by Washington.

The Ecuadorians suffered a variety of ailments immediately following the spraying, including intestinal pain and vomiting, diarrhoea, headaches, dizziness, numbness, burning of eyes or skin, blurred vision, difficulty in breathing and rashes, says the study, which is to be published in the journal *Genetics and Molecular Biology*.

But the extensive damage to DNA (deoxyribonucleic acid) found in the randomly selected individuals may activate the

131

development of cancer or other developmental effects resulting in miscarriages, according to lead researcher César Paz y Miño, head of human molecular genetics at the Catholic University of Ecuador.

Measured at greater than twenty times the maximum recommended rate, the increased concentration levels of Roundup may be causing genetic mutations.

In general, everyone has some level of DNA damage due to exposure to ultraviolet radiation, air pollution, toxic chemicals, and other factors. However, none of the twenty-four randomly selected individuals used tobacco, alcohol or non-prescription drugs, nor did they use other herbicides or pesticides that could have caused the extensive DNA damage observed, Paz y Miño told *Tierramérica*.

Increased Spraying Raises Health Concerns

The concentration levels of Roundup were measured at more than twenty times the maximum recommended rate and may be the reason behind the genotoxic (capable of causing genetic mutation) effect on the exposed individuals, he said.

The blood samples were collected by Spanish doctor Adolfo Maldonado, of the nongovernmental [organization] Acción Ecológica, which since the beginning of this decade has been studying health, economic and social problems of Ecuadorian populations affected by the aerial herbicide spraying in neighbouring Colombia.

Washington has been financing since 2000 the aerial spraying in Colombia of coca crops—the raw material of cocaine, of which Colombia is the world's leading producer. In the past three years, it has spent more than 1.3 billion dollars to combat the drug trade.

In 2006, the Colombian National Police's Anti-Narcotics Directorate (DIRAN) sprayed 171,613 hectares [unit of land equal to 100 ares or 2.471 acres] of illicit coca and opium poppy, according to a March 2007 International Narcotics Control Strategy Report released by the U.S. State Department.

The extent of aerial spraying has increased every year since 2000, with 24 percent more in 2006 than 2005.

Three aerial spraying units, funded and operated by the United States, work full-time in Colombia, and a fourth unit was added in 2006, the report notes.

Aerial spraying "follows strict environmental safeguards, monitored permanently by several GOC (government of Colombia) agencies," it says.

As for impacts on health, "the Colombian National Institute of Health has not verified a single case of adverse human health effects linked to glyphosate spraying," states the report.

Paz y Miño disputes that assertion. In addition to his own study, there are studies from the University of the Andes and from the National University of Colombia that also "report the damage that the aerial sprayings produces in Colombians," he said.

In fact, since 1994 there have been many studies that show potential health impacts of Roundup on people and wildlife, he said.

Roundup is a mixture of glyphosate and other chemicals designed to increase the herbicide's penetration into plants or boost its toxic effects.

But only glyphosate—the active ingredient—has been fully tested by U.S. regulators for its health and environmental effects.

Research Points to Evidence of Genetic Damage

In 2005, a team of French scientists headed by Gilles-Eric Seralin reported that Roundup was toxic to human placental cells within hours of exposure, at levels ten times lower than those found in agricultural use.

Just last month [March 2008], Serelin reported new findings which show that even diluted up to 10,000 times, the chemical disrupted hormone production in placental cells.

"This work may be of help in better understating the problems of miscarriages, premature births or sexual malformations of babies," Seralin said in a statement.

In April of this year, DNA damage was also documented by Turkish scientists at Mersin University. The DNA of fish was damaged even at extremely low levels of five to fifteen parts per million of Roundup.

"There is no doubt that the spraying programme is killing amphibians in Colombia," said Rick Relyea, a biologist at the University of Pittsburgh, in the northeastern U.S. state of Pennsylvania.

In 2005, Relyea documented that Roundup was lethal to frogs. More than 90 percent of the tadpoles exposed to small doses were killed by a chemical called polyethoxylated tallowamine (POEA), which is part of normal Roundup formulation. POEA allows glyphosate to penetrate plant leaves.

"Destruction of legal crops, death of domestic animals and fish in hatcheries, in addition to the human health impacts, have all been documented."

Experiments with frogs in the United States showed that "more than 80 percent of the adults exposed to Roundup spray at normal rates died in a day." There is no data about the impacts of the spraying of Colombian frogs and amphibians.

Those findings prompted the U.S. Congress to obtain guarantees in 2006 that wetlands would not be sprayed in Colombia, Relyea told *Tierramérica*.

Ecuador Sues Colombia over Fumigations

The government of Ecuador today [March 31, 2008] filed suit . . . against the government of Colombia, in an effort to stop or restrict aerial anti-coca spraying that has allegedly sickened people on the Ecuadorean side of the border and harmed livestock, farmland, and sensitive, ecologically diverse rain forest areas. . . .

[A]nnouncing the lawsuit, Ecuadorean Foreign Minister María Isabel Salvador said, "There is no doubt that the fumigations conducted by the government of Colombia constitute a grave violation of the sovereignty of Ecuador and of the most basic principles of international law."

Environment News Service (ENS), *"Ecuador Sues Colombia to Stop Anti-Coca Herbicide Spray,"* March 31, 2008.

However, most frogs live in small wetlands that aren't easily detected from the air and many species in the region are found in trees and grasslands, he said.

As Roundup is the most widely used herbicide in the world, it may be a factor [in] the dramatic global decline in frogs, but there is no firm proof, Relyea says.

But there is ample proof of the effects of aerial spraying along the Ecuadorian border, says Paz y Miño.

Destruction of legal crops, death of domestic animals and fish in hatcheries, in addition to the human health impacts, have all been documented.

His research group is finishing a new set of studies on the effects of glyphosate, alone or with POEA, on insects and in vitro cultured human cells, he said.

"I could tell you, in advance, that we have found (genetic) damage in these."

Colombia and Afghanistan Are Potential Targets for a Dangerous Biologically Engineered Fungus

John Otis

In the following viewpoint, John Otis investigates controversy brewing over the use of mycoherbicides to eradicate illicit drug crops such as opium in Afghanistan and coca in Colombia. Some members of the United States Congress are pushing for a bill to use a fungus known as Fusarium oxysporum, *believing that it will help them win the war on drugs, while opponents worry that this mycoherbicide could mutate and destroy other plant life in its path—legal food crops, for instance. Some even believe using mycoherbicides would put the United States on the verge of biological warfare. Journalist John Otis is the South American bureau chief for the* Houston Chronicle, *based in Bogotá, Colombia.*

As you read, consider the following questions:

1. According to the author, why have U.S.-sponsored eradication efforts been failing?

2. How do mycoherbicides work to destroy plants, as explained in the following article?

John Otis, "A Controversial Weapon in the War Against Drugs," *Houston Chronicle*, January 18, 2007. Reproduced by permission by the publisher, conveyed through Copyright Clearance Center, Inc.

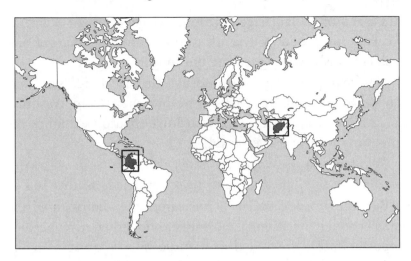

3. Why did President Bill Clinton's administration in 2000 waive the use of mycoherbicides in Colombia?

Is it a silver bullet in the war on drugs or an outlawed biological weapon?

Frustrated by the nonstop flow of cocaine and heroin into the United States, some American lawmakers are promoting mycoherbicides, weed killers made from toxic, mold-like fungi that they believe could be used to eliminate illegal drug crops for good.

For years, mycoherbicides had been largely written off by many U.S. officials. They were concerned the fungi could mutate to kill legitimate crops and that their use overseas would violate the United Nations' 31-year-old Biological Weapons Convention and other treaties.

"The DEA [Drug Enforcement Administration] doesn't want to touch this with a ten-foot pole," said Eric Rosenquist, a leading expert on mycoherbicides at the Agriculture Department's [USDA] Research Service.

Still, a handful of determined Congress members have kept the issue alive. Last month [December 2006] they inserted into a bill authorizing funding for the White House drug czar's office language that requires government scientists to carry out a new round of studies into mycoherbicides. President Bush later signed the bill into law.

"I'm telling you, the war on drugs ain't working," said Rep. Dan Burton, R-Ind., in a telephone interview from Washington. "And if it ain't working, you don't sit around doing the same thing over and over again.

"We have to use whatever tools that we think will work and that are safe," he said, "and mycoherbicides fit that bill."

Burton, Sen. Joe Biden, D-Del., now the chairman of the Senate Foreign Relations Committee, and other mycoherbide supporters are dismayed over a surge in Afghanistan in the production of opium poppies, which are used to make heroin, and bumper crops of South American coca, the key ingredient in cocaine. Afghanistan provides about 90 percent of the world's opiates, while Colombia is the source of 80 to 90 percent of the global cocaine supply.

U.S.-sponsored programs to chop down poppy and coca fields or fumigate them with chemical herbicides have made little dent because drug farmers have moved elsewhere to plant more. Much of the U.S.-bound cocaine comes across the Texas-Mexico border, and is often routed through Houston, a city U.S. law enforcement officials describe as a leading cocaine distribution center for the rest of the United States.

Some Believe Mycoherbicides Are Key to Drug War Success

Since the 1970s, when a fungus called *Fusarium oxysporum* was found to kill coca plants in Hawaii, scientists for the CIA [Central Intelligence Agency] and the U.S. Departments of Energy and Agriculture have carried out research—often in secret—to develop fungal herbicides to combat drug plantations.

Called mycoherbicides, they work by producing toxic compounds that dissolve the cell walls of targeted plants. Unlike traditional herbicides, mycoherbicides can reproduce themselves and linger in the soil for many years to destroy replanted crops. Some view them as an environmentally friendly alternative to chemical herbicides, a sort of "Agent Green."

"Mycoherbicides are so controversial that U.S. government scientists have not tested them outside of carefully controlled greenhouses and have not found a nation willing to spray them on drug crops."

"If proven to be successful, mycoherbicides could revolutionize our drug eradication efforts," Rep. Mark Souder, R-Ind., the former chairman of the House drug policy subcommittee, told reporters in Washington.

But mycoherbicides are so controversial that U.S. government scientists have not tested them outside of carefully controlled greenhouses and have not found a nation willing to spray them on drug crops.

Fusarium oxysporum, for example, comes from a family that includes hundreds of fungi that can attack everything from corn to watermelons. One strain of *Fusarium wilt* [plant disease] is responsible for the current epidemic killing Los Angeles's iconic palm trees.

In 1999, Florida's secretary of environmental protection rejected a proposal to use *Fusarium oxysporum* to attack the state's marijuana crop due to fears that the mycoherbicide could mutate and destroy legitimate crops like tomatoes, peppers, and flowers.

"Ask any U.S. farmer what he thinks about using mycoherbicides and spreading them around, and his eyes will bulge out of his head," said Sanho Tree, a drug policy expert at [the] Institute for Policy Studies in Washington.

Mycoherbicide Testing Met with Challenge

Searching for a test site, the U.S. Congress in 2000 conditioned the delivery of a $1.3 billion package of mostly anti-drug aid for Colombia to the [capital] Bogotá government's commitment to test mycoherbicides on coca and opium crops.

But Colombia refused. As opposition to the plant killer dubbed the "Franken-fungus" [Frankenstein-like, destructive and difficult to control] intensified here, the Clinton administration waived the mycoherbicide provision due to concerns that it would be accused of promoting biological warfare. Meanwhile, Bolivia, Peru, and Ecuador all banned drug eradication through chemical or biological means.

In 2002, the United Nations [UN] abandoned a U.S.-financed study of mycoherbicides in Uzbekistan amid resistance to using a biological agent to combat that country's opium poppy crop. Since then, no further research on mycoherbicides by UN agencies or the U.S. government has gone forward, according to Thomas Schweich, the number two official at the State Department's Bureau for International Narcotics and Law Enforcement Affairs.

"We determined that there was absolutely no place that we could field test mycoherbicides because of the resistance," Schweich told a congressional hearing in March [2006].

The DEA refused to comment on mycoherbicides. But U.S. drug czar John Walters voiced skepticism when questioned by Burton at a congressional hearing about using *Fusarium oxysporum* on Colombia's coca fields.

"If you were to (use) it and it is not specific to coca, it could cause considerable damage to the environment, which in Colombia is very delicate," Walters said.

Even so, the language in last month's congressional bill requires Walters's office to work with government scientists in studying the feasibility of using *Fusarium oxysporum* and other mycoherbicides on drug plants. It's unclear how much the tests will cost, but they will likely take several years to complete.

Mycoherbicide Fungus Poses Toxic Threat to Environment, Humans

The once-secret mycoherbicide program . . . was first proposed during the 1970s and sounded like a good idea to naive do-gooders and unschooled drug warriors. The government would develop a fungus that would only attack certain drug plants; it would be specific, and leave everything else healthy. . . .

But the devil, as always, is in the details: the fungus does not just grab the target plant and wrestle it to the ground: . . . The mycoherbicide fungus acts as a living micro-chemical factory, producing toxic compounds called mycotoxins that it itself is immune to . . . which dissolve the target's cell walls. The fungus then ingests the liquefied contents of the target cell and reproduces itself, moving into the dead cell space as an uninvited and deadly guest. . . .

The cell-dissolving "mycotoxins" that are produced by the proposed mycoherbicides were initially discovered after hundreds of thousands of people died due to internal hemorrhaging after eating bread made from *Fusarium*-contaminated overwintered grain during the mid-1940s in the Soviet Union. . . . During the Cold War . . . mycotoxins were "weaponized," mass-produced, and stockpiled . . . for use in chemical warfare.

Another trichothecene toxin, fumonisin, was in the news a couple of years ago because Hispanic mothers had been eating *Fusarium*-contaminated corn tortillas. This resulted in a rash of children born brainless and with other birth defects along the Rio Grande River.

Jeremy Bigwood, "Mycoherbicide Redux: U.S. Congressmen Declare Biological War on South America in New Antidrug Proposal," The Narco News Bulletin, *July 15, 2005. www.narconews.com.*

"Our judgement at the moment is that the case for myco-herbicides is not proven," said David Murray, a scientist and one of Walters's deputies. "If there is a change in the evidence, we might revisit the issue."

Dr. Rosenquist, the USDA expert, doubts that will happen. When he tested *Fusarium oxysporum* in the 1990s, he had to inundate coca plants with the mycoherbicide, using more than twenty pounds of active ingredient per acre—and even then, only thirty to forty percent of the bushes died.

"Why would you want to use something that doesn't work very well?" he said.

Periodical Bibliography

The following articles have been selected to supplement the diverse views presented in this chapter.

ABC 7 News, KGO	"Mexican Drug Lords in Area National Forests?" September 18, 2006. http://abclocal.go.com.
Paul V. Beddoe	"Meth Lab Cleanup Bill Now Law," National Association of Counties (NACO), Meth Action Clearinghouse, December 24, 2007. www.naco.org.
Drug Policy Alliance Network	"Don't Let Congress Poison People," April 4, 2006. www.drugpolicy.org.
Drug War Facts	"Environment," May 21, 2007. www.drugwarfacts.org.
Living on Earth	"Colombia: An Environment Under Siege," 2008. www.loe.org.
Douglas Quan	"The Labs: Experts Still Unsure What Level of Post-Cleanup Residue Is Safe," *The Press-Enterprise*, May 17, 2008. www.pe.com.
Paul Rogers	"Woes Linger for California's Parks," *Santa Cruz Sentinel*, May 27, 2008. www.santacruzsentinel.com.
Transnational Institute	"Plan Afghanistan," *Drug Policy Briefing No. 10*, February 2005. www.tni.org.
U.S. Department of State. Embassy of the United States—Phnom Penh, Cambodia	"Cambodia Begins Cleanup of Meth 'Super Lab' with U.S. Assistance," August 16, 2007. http://cambodia.usembassy.gov.
Washington Office on Latin America (WOLA)	"Evaluating Mycoherbicides for Illicit Drug Crop Control," April 27, 2007. www.wola.org.

CHAPTER 4

Alternative Policies to Prohibition

Legalization Is the Only Viable Option to Drug Prohibition

Jeffrey A. Miron

In the following viewpoint, Jeffrey A. Miron argues against prohibition, believing that it has caused significant harm to society. He explores whether changes to prohibition could improve current policy and makes a case for full legalization. Miron is a senior lecturer and director of undergraduate studies in the Department of Economics at Harvard University; in addition, he is a research associate for the National Bureau of Economic Research. With an emphasis in libertarianism and the economics of illicit drugs, Miron has written numerous publications including books, articles in refereed journals, and editorials for the Boston Herald, Boston Business Journal, *and* Boston Globe.

As you read, consider the following questions:

1. How many states decriminalized marijuana in the 1970s?

2. According to Miron, what potential problem could occur if the limits on prescribing drugs under a policy of medicalization are too strict?

3. Why do governments struggle in promoting needle exchange programs, according to the author?

Jeffrey A. Miron, "Alternatives to Prohibition and Other Policies Toward Drugs," *Drug War Crimes: The Consequences of Prohibition*, Oakland, CA: The Independent Institute, 2004, pp. 75–83. Copyright © 2004 by The Independent Institute. Reproduced by permission of The Independent Institute, 100 Swan Way, Oakland, CA 94021-1428 USA, www.independent.org.

Although certain modifications of prohibition are likely an improvement over current policy, full legalization is better still.... Assuming drugs are legal, [are] auxiliary policies toward drugs such as subsidized treatment, needle exchanges, drug testing, or sin taxation likely to increase economic well-being[?] The conclusion is that some of these policies might reduce the harms from drug consumption, and legalization combined with these policies is certainly an improvement over prohibition. But these policies generate their own costs, and there is no compelling reason they are better than simply legalizing drugs and treating them like other goods.

Increased Enforcement Would Not Reduce Drug Use

One alternative to current prohibition is a regime with similar laws but a substantially different level of enforcement. Drug arrest rates, drug violation incarceration rates, expenditure on enforcement, asset seizures, and other measures of enforcement have changed substantially over time within the United States and vary widely across countries.

A key consideration in determining the optimal level of enforcement is that such activities likely exhibit decreasing marginal returns in reducing drug consumption. Cost-effective law enforcement addresses the easiest targets first, implying a diminishing marginal effect of enforcement in raising price. Moreover, any increase in price tends to yield diminishing returns in reducing consumption, since casual consumers have cheap substitutes like alcohol and tobacco available and thus relatively elastic demands, while heavy users have less elastic demands. As price rises, the latter group makes up a higher proportion of the market, meaning further increases in price have minimal impact on drug use....

Thus, whereas many prohibitionists believe present levels of enforcement are "inadequate," there is little evidence that increased enforcement would reduce drug use further....

A Case for Legalizing "Hard" Drugs?

A second possible modification of current prohibition is legalization of marijuana only. Many legalization advocates focus on marijuana, and in many places, enforcement of marijuana prohibition is less severe than enforcement of prohibition for other drugs. The Netherlands, for example, practices grudging tolerance toward "soft" drugs (e.g., marijuana and hashish) combined with a more punitive approach toward "hard" drugs (e.g., cocaine and heroin).

If the only objective of drug policy is to reduce myopic [imprudent] or externality-causing drug consumption, the case for legalizing marijuana is perhaps stronger than that for legalizing cocaine, opiates, or other illicit drugs. Although the health risks of all these drugs are frequently exaggerated, cocaine, opiates, and other drugs have a greater potential for serious adverse consequences than does marijuana. For example, both cocaine and heroin can cause fatal overdoses, but this outcome is essentially unknown for marijuana.

"Decriminalization does not reduce violent crime, improve product quality, eliminate corruption, avoid transfers to criminals, prevent the erosion of civil liberties, or ameliorate most other negatives of prohibition."

Nevertheless, the analysis above emphasizes that most negative consequences associated with drugs derive from their prohibition rather than from their consumption. Contrary to popular views, drugs do not differ radically from a range of other commodities, and their distinctive characteristics do not explain the effects of drug prohibition on the market for drugs. The markets for commodities that display similar characteristics but are not prohibited (like cigarettes and coffee) fail to exhibit the features of the market for illicit drugs. Conversely, the markets for commodities that do not display these characteristics but that are often prohibited (like gambling and prostitution) exhibit many of the same negative features as the market for drugs. Thus, the case for legalizing cocaine, heroin, and other hard drugs is as strong as that for marijuana.

Decriminalization Ineffective When Transactions Remain Illegal

A different alternative to current prohibition is decriminalization. As usually defined, decriminalization means eliminating criminal penalties for possession of small amounts of drugs while maintaining penalties against trafficking or possession of larger amounts. Opponents of prohibition usually suggest decriminalization for marijuana. Eleven U.S. states decriminalized marijuana in the 1970s, and a number of European countries have decriminalized marijuana more recently. A few of these countries have also decriminalized other drugs.

Many critics of drug prohibition advocate decriminalization as a superior approach. Decriminalization does reduce the adverse legal consequences of prohibition for users. But because transactions in a decriminalized market are illegal, there is still a black market with all the attendant ills. Thus, decriminalization does not reduce violent crime, improve product quality, eliminate corruption, avoid transfers to criminals, prevent the erosion of civil liberties, or ameliorate most other negatives of prohibition. And it is logically awkward, at a minimum, for society to say that possession and use of drugs are legal but production and sale are not. . . .

Medicalization Shows Some Promise as Policy

Still a different alternative to prohibition, which might be termed medicalization, is to put control over drugs in the hands of physicians, with little or no oversight from law enforcement. Under current U.S. policy, doctors can prescribe most opiates, cocaine, amphetamines, and depressants, but their ability to prescribe is strictly limited, and they cannot prescribe drugs such as heroin, marijuana, and LSD under any circumstance. More broadly, even when doctors can prescribe controlled substances, they avoid doing so because of concern about legal monitoring of their prescription practices. Under a less restrictive, medical approach, which exists to some degree in Europe, doctors would face minimal legal restraint on their prescribing practices. In particular, they might be allowed to "maintain" addicts by prescribing continued supplies of opiates or other drugs as the "treatment" for addiction.

The critical effect of medicalization is to provide many drug users with a legal supply, thereby reducing the black market. If the restraints on doctors are minimal, some physicians will prescribe freely, potentially reducing the black market to insignificance. Thus, from the perspective of eliminating the negative effects of a prohibition-induced black market, medicalization is beneficial. It is not obvious this approach is better than legalization. If the limits on prescribing are mild, medicalization is little different from de facto [in practice, but not official by law] legalization. If the limits are strict, substantial numbers of drug consumers will be unable to obtain drugs via medical channels and support the black market instead. The critical issue is that medicalization reduces the degree of enforcement.

Policies Toward Drugs Under Legalization

Although various modifications of prohibition are an improvement over current policy, none is obviously better than simply legalizing drugs. Given this conclusion, the remaining question is whether policy should attempt to ameliorate those negatives consequences of drugs that might occur under legalization. Many such policies already exist, but they are logically separable from the issue of prohibition versus legalization and can potentially continue if drugs are legal.

Drug Abuse Treatment. One policy that might reduce the negative consequences of drug use is government-subsidized drug-abuse treatment. The desired effect of subsidies is to increase the number of persons receiving treatment, thereby reducing the quantity of drug use and especially the adverse effects of drug abuse. . . .

Subsidizing drug-abuse treatment raises a number of issues. Although it is easy to advocate this policy out of compassion for drug abusers, the question for society is whether the benefits, such as increased earnings for drug users or lower crime committed by users, exceed the costs. . . . An additional issue is that subsidizing drug treatment might encourage drug use, and even the perception that this occurs—or a feeling by some that subsidizing treatment "rewards" drug use—is a problematic consequence of this policy.

None of these caveats means that treatment never works. The point is that subsidizing treatment is a separate question from whether treatment is beneficial, and it is a separate question from whether prohibition is preferable to legalization. Many critics of prohibition take as given that reduced expenditure for prohibition should translate into increased expenditure for subsidized treatment. It might be desirable to both legalize drugs and subsidize treatment, but subsidized treatment has its own costs and requires independent analysis.

Needle Exchange Programs. A different way that policy might attempt to reduce the harms of drug use under legalization is via needle exchanges, in which private or government groups provide clean needles to addicts who otherwise share dirty needles and thereby spread HIV and other diseases. There is some evidence these programs reduce needle sharing and little evidence they encourage drug use. These programs currently operate in a number of U.S. cities and several foreign countries.

Needle exchanges plausibly reduce the harms associated with drug use, but these programs exist in substantial part because of government restrictions on the sale of clean needles, which in turn reflect prohibition. If drugs were legal, there would be far fewer restrictions on nonprescription needle sales. Thus, there is no obvious benefit to such programs under legalization; governments could simply repeal the prohibitions on sales of clean needles, allowing private groups greater freedom to run needle exchanges. In addition, drug prices would be lower under legalization, which would reduce the incentive to inject drugs and thereby diminish any "need" for government needle exchanges. Beyond these considerations, needle exchanges are an awkward activity for the government since they appear to sanction or even subsidize drug use. Even under legalization, this activity is likely to be controversial.

Education. Further policies that might alleviate the harms of drugs under legalization are government media or school-based campaigns that provide information about the consequences of drug use. Other things equal, more information is better, and persuading people not to use drugs circumvents most other issues. But this is not the right benchmark for gauging government anti-drug campaigns. In many cases these exaggerate the dangers of drug use to such a degree that the audience ignores the message entirely. . . .

Drug Testing. Yet another policy that is currently employed to ameliorate the negative effects of drug use is government-mandated drug testing. This policy allegedly reduces the frequency of workplace accidents and improves employee productivity. Alternatively, testing can help employers screen out irresponsible or poorly motivated employees. There is nothing wrong with testing per se, but there is no reason for government to mandate this practice. Employers face appropriate incentives to balance the improvement in productivity that might accompany testing against the costs of carrying out the tests. . . .

Decriminalization

In the context of drugs, the word "decriminalization" entered the popular lexicon during the 1970s and described changes to the marijuana laws in eleven states. The changes were modest. Under them, marijuana remained illegal under both state and federal law, and one could still be prosecuted and punished for simple possession of marijuana. The difference was that such possession of a small quantity was no longer an offense under state law for which one could lose one's liberty (i.e., be arrested) upon being caught. And, typically, such charges did not carry the risk of creating a permanent criminal record. As a result, prosecutions for marijuana were said to resemble prosecutions for speeding or other traffic offenses—offenders were given a ticket and fine and possibly had to appear in court, but they were not arrested on the spot and taken in.

In terms of a policy alternative to prohibition, such decriminalization represented a mere tinkering with the statutory law, not any major policy change. It was merely a kinder, gentler version of prohibition.

Richard M. Evans and Stanley Neustadter,
"Legalization: An Introduction," Drugs and Society:
U.S. Public Policy, *ed. Jefferson M. Fish, 2006.*

Advertising Restrictions. One more policy that might exist in a legalized drug market is restrictions on advertising, such as those currently in effect for tobacco. The assumption behind such policies is that advertising induces people to consume the advertised commodity, but existing evidence does not justify such an assumption. Instead, advertising of mature products mainly affects which brand consumers choose, given they have already decided to consume. . . .

Drug Taxes. A final way that government might address the harms of drug use within a legalized market is by imposing a tax on drugs in excess of that on other goods. Most economies impose "sin taxes" on various commodities, including tobacco, alcohol, and gasoline. The use of taxes to discourage drug consumption faces an important constraint: the tax must not be so high that it generates a black market. . . .

By reducing consumption, sin taxation potentially reduces externalities and myopic consumption. Whether sin taxation is superior to legalization depends in part on the magnitude of externalities relative to irrational consumption.

Legalization Is Best Option

Although many variations on current prohibition are plausibly beneficial, simple legalization appears even better. Second, within a legalization regime, auxiliary policies might improve welfare, but there is no compelling evidence for any of these interventions.

The United Kingdom Should Decriminalize Drugs

Kailash Chand

In the following viewpoint, Kailash Chand, a general practitioner, argues for the decriminalization of drugs in the United Kingdom. According to Chand, prohibition drives crime, and the illegal status of drugs only creates harm for users who need safer alternatives and rehabilitation programs. Believing that adult drug users should be free to make their own choices, Chand asserts that users should not be marginalized as criminals. He instead argues for a policy of regulated legalization, maintaining that users should be able to purchase safer drugs and have treatment options readily available.

As you read, consider the following questions:

1. According to Chand, how has decriminalization helped drug addicts in the Netherlands?
2. What does Chand believe to be the best "weapon" to combat drug problems today?
3. How does making drugs illegal increase the risk of harm for young people today, according to the author?

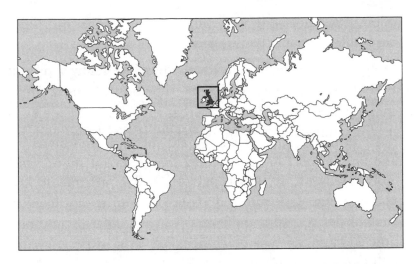

There is a way that the UK [United Kingdom] government could more than halve the prison population, prevent burglaries and prostitution, rip the heart out of organised crime, and free up millions of hours of police time. Yet politicians, terrified of the rightwing press, would never dare to suggest the legalisation, regulation, and control of the drugs market, even though it could save lives and bring an end to the needless criminalisation of some of the most vulnerable members of our society. Even downgrading cannabis—a tiny step in the right direction—is now being reconsidered.

Prohibition vs. Decriminalisation

Prohibition as a policy has failed. Just look at the US, where hundreds of thousands of people have been jailed and, despite billions of pounds of funding for draconian [strict, severe] policies, higher purity drugs continue to flood the market.

Many of the violent criminal gangs owe their existence to the burgeoning, underground drug market. It is they—and not the governments—who control this trade and it is their turf wars that fuel gun crime. Transform—an influential drug policy foundation that has campaigned against prohibition—reports that the annual trade controlled by the gangs is more than £100bn [billion]. It also points to the fact that the policy drives crime among desperate low-income addicts.

You only have to walk through the UK's many red light districts to see the effect of heroin addiction. Young women, putting themselves at grave danger, as they sell their bodies in return for enough cash to fund their next hit. Then there are the prisons overflowing.

Decriminalising drugs has paid off in the Netherlands. Decriminalisation of heroin and other hard drugs has allowed addicts to be treated as patients. As a result hardly any new heroin addicts are registered, while existing users are supported and have been helped to get jobs.

Drugs could easily be regulated in the same manner that alcohol and tobacco are regulated and, more importantly, heavily taxed. The price could still be substantially less than current prices on the illicit market, and the revenue generated from the regulation could then be funnelled into education and other rehabilitation programmes. Educating children at an early age is the best weapon we have to combat the drug problems we face today. It would give children the tools to make intelligent and healthy choices in the future. And instead of turning drug addicts back to the streets, investing in rehabilitation programmes would not only help the addicts, but help society.

"A sensible policy of regulation and control would reduce burglary, cut gun crime, bring women off the streets, clear out our overflowing prisons, and raise billions in tax revenues."

Many people may think that taking drugs is inherently wrong and so should be illegal. But there is a question of effectiveness—does making it illegal stop people doing it? The

The Treatment of Users of High-Harm-Causing Drugs

At any one time, over 220,000 high-harm-causing drug users are not engaged in treatment.

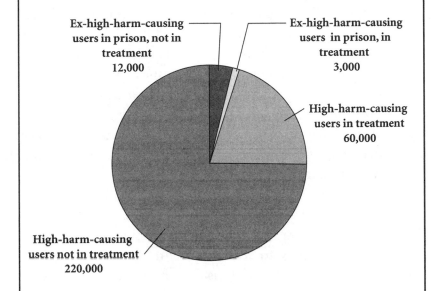

Ex-high-harm-causing users in prison, not in treatment **12,000**

Ex-high-harm-causing users in prison, in treatment **3,000**

High-harm-causing users in treatment **60,000**

High-harm-causing users not in treatment **220,000**

TAKEN FROM: Cabinet Office, The Strategy Unit, "Strategy Unit Drugs Report, Phase One: Understanding the Issues," May 12, 2003.

answer is clearly no. One could even argue that legalisation would eliminate part of the attraction of taking drugs—the allure of doing something illegal.

Increased Harm

The illegal status adds to the dangers of drug taking. Instead of buying a joint from a safe outlet where the toxicity can be monitored and maintained, a young person who wants to smoke cannabis has to take to the streets and buy it from a violent dealer, who suggests that she instead tries ecstasy, crack cocaine, or heroin. Moreover, all that is available (so I am told in many cities) is super strong varieties such as skunk. Purity of cocaine in the UK has fallen steeply as suppliers cut the drugs with other substances. And over 70 people in the UK died from a single dose of bacterially infected heroin in 2000. Regulation could control the process and greatly reduce the dangers of impure drugs.

Then there is the bloody chain back to the original supplier. Countries like Afghanistan, Colombia, and Jamaica have had their economies rocked and destabilised by the illegal market while bribery, corruption, and conflict have ruled.

In the UK we have cut off huge swathes [portions] of the population, branding them criminals and creating an underclass of people who no longer feel part of our society. A sensible policy of regulation and control would reduce burglary, cut gun crime, bring women off the streets, clear out our overflowing prisons, and raise billions in tax revenues. Drug users could buy from places where they could be sure the drugs had not been cut with dangerous, cost-saving chemicals. There would be clear information about the risks involved and guidance on how to seek treatment. It is time to allow adults the freedom to make decisions about the harmful substances they consume.

The United Kingdom Should Not Decriminalize Drugs

Joseph A. Califano Jr.

In the following viewpoint, Joseph A. Califano Jr. argues against decriminalization and legalization of illicit drugs in the United Kingdom, maintaining that such policies will make harmful drugs more accessible and acceptable. Califano believes that drug abuse is increasing crime and creating problems in the health care system. Children and teenagers should be protected from drug availability, he argues, praising Sweden's approach to drug control. Califano is chairman of the National Center on Addiction and Substance Abuse at Columbia University. A Harvard Law School graduate, he has held many positions in the United States government, including senior domestic policy aide to President Lyndon B. Johnson and Secretary of Health, Education, and Welfare under President Jimmy Carter.

As you read, consider the following questions:

1. Why does Califano feel that it is unrealistic to expect that drugs can be regulated like alcohol and cigarettes—legal for adult use only?

2. According to the author, what negative consequence occurred when, in 2005, the government in Britain extended hours of operation for pubs?

Joseph A. Califano Jr., "Should Drugs Be Decriminalised? No," *British Medical Journal*, vol. 335, no. 7627, November 10, 2007, p. 967. www.bmj.com. Copyright © 2007 British Medical Association. Reproduced by permission.

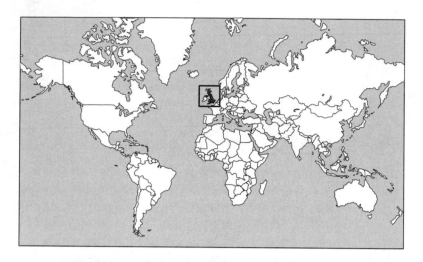

3. How is the marijuana today different than it was in the early 1980s, according to Califano?

Drug misuse (usually called abuse in the United States) infects the world's criminal justice, health care, and social service systems. Although bans on the import, manufacture, sale, and possession of drugs such as marijuana, cocaine, and heroin should remain, drug policies do need a fix. Neither legalisation nor decriminalisation is the answer. Rather, more resources and energy should be devoted to research, prevention, and treatment, and each citizen and institution should take responsibility to combat all substance misuse and addiction.

"What we don't need is legalisation or decriminalisation, which will make illegal drugs cheaper, easier to obtain, and more acceptable to use. . . . Drugs are not dangerous because they are illegal; they are illegal because they are dangerous."

Vigorous and intelligent enforcement of criminal law makes drugs harder to get and more expensive. Sensible use of courts, punishment, and prisons can encourage misusers to enter treatment and thus reduce crime. Why not treat a teenager arrested for marijuana use in the same way that the United States treats someone arrested for drink-driving when no injury occurs? See the arrest as an opportunity and require the teenager to be screened, have any needed treatment, and attend sessions to learn about the dangers of marijuana use.

The medical profession and the public health community should educate society that addiction is a complex physical, psychological, emotional, and spiritual disease, not a moral failing or easily abandoned act of self indulgence. Children should receive education and prevention programmes that take into account cultural and sex differences and are relevant to their age. We should make effective treatment available to all who need it and establish high standards of training for treatment providers. Social service programmes, such as those to help abused children and homeless people, should confront the drug and alcohol misuse and addiction commonly involved, rather than ignore or hide it because of the associated stigma.

Availability Is the Mother of Use

What we don't need is legalisation or decriminalisation, which will make illegal drugs cheaper, easier to obtain, and more acceptable to use. The United States has some 60 million smokers, up to 20 million alcoholics and alcohol misusers, but only around 6 million illegal drug addicts. If illegal drugs were easier to obtain, this figure would rise.

Switzerland's "needle park," touted as a way to restrict a few hundred heroin users to a small area, turned into a grotesque tourist attraction of 20,000 addicts and had to be closed before it infected the entire city of Zurich. Italy, where personal possession of a few doses of drugs like heroin has generally been exempt from criminal sanction, has one of the highest rates of heroin addiction in Europe, with more than 60% of AIDS cases there attributable to intravenous drug use.

Most legalisation advocates say they would legalise drugs only for adults. Our experience with tobacco and alcohol shows that keeping drugs legal "for adults only" is an impossible dream. Teenage smoking and drinking are widespread in the United States, the United Kingdom, and Europe.

The Netherlands established "coffee shops," where customers could select types of marijuana just as they might choose ice cream flavours. Between 1984 and 1992, adolescent use nearly tripled. Responding to international pressure and the outcry from its own citizens, the Dutch government reduced the number of marijuana shops and the amount that could be sold and raised the age for admission from 16 to 18. In 2007, the Dutch government announced plans to ban the sale of hallucinogenic mushrooms.

Restriction

Recent events in Britain highlight the importance of curbing availability. In 2005, the government extended the hours of operation for pubs, with some allowed to serve 24 hours a day. Rather than curbing binge drinking, the result has been a sharp increase in crime between 3 A.M. and 6 A.M., in violent crimes in certain pubs, and in emergency treatment for alcohol misusers.

Sweden offers an example of a successful restrictive drug policy. Faced with rising drug use in the 1990s, the government tightened drug control, stepped up police action, mounted a national action plan, and created a national drug coordinator. The result: "Drug use is just a third of the European average."

Almost daily we learn more about marijuana's addictive and dangerous characteristics. Today's teenagers' pot is far more potent than their parents' pot. The average amount of tetrahydrocannabinol, the psychoactive ingredient in mari-

Use of Marijuana and Serious Mental Illness

Among persons aged 18 or older, those who first used marijuana before age 12 were twice as likely to have serious mental illness in the past year as those who first used marijuana at age 18 or older.

Office of Applied Studies,
"Age at First Use of Marijuana and Past Year Serious Mental Illness,"
The NSDUH Report, *May 3, 2005. www.oas.samhsa.gov.*

juana, in seized samples in the United States has more than doubled since 1983. Antonio Maria Costa, director of the UN [United Nations] Office on Drugs and Crime (UNODC), has warned, "Today, the harmful characteristics of cannabis are no longer that different from those of other plant-based drugs such as cocaine and heroin."

Evidence that cannabis use can cause serious mental illness is mounting. A study published in the *Lancet* "found a consistent increase in incidence of psychosis outcomes in people who had used cannabis." The study prompted the journal's editors to retract their 1995 statement that, "smoking of cannabis, even long term, is not harmful to health."

Drugs are not dangerous because they are illegal; they are illegal because they are dangerous. A child who reaches age 21 without smoking, misusing alcohol, or using illegal drugs is virtually certain to never do so. Today, most children don't use illicit drugs, but all of them, particularly the poorest, are vulnerable to misuse and addiction. Legalisation and decriminalisation—policies certain to increase illegal drug availability and use among our children—hardly qualify as public health approaches.

The Netherlands Demonstrates Temperance Through Decriminalization

Andrew Stuttaford

On his tour through Amsterdam, Andrew Stuttaford provides a firsthand look into the Netherlands' liberal policy on soft drugs, where coffee shops are licensed to sell small quantities of cannabis to adults over the age of 18. While many critics argue that marijuana is a "gateway drug" leading to harder drugs, supporters of Dutch policy argue that regulation reduces harm for users since they are able to use soft drugs responsibly without being criminalized or forced into illegal circles where the risk to experiment with hard drugs, like heroin, has proven to be much greater. Stuttaford is a contributing editor to National Review *and a writer for the* New York Sun.

As you read, consider the following questions:

1. What is the age requirement for smoking marijuana in the Netherlands?

2. Having been reduced from thirty grams in recent years, what is the current purchase limit for marijuana in the Netherlands?

3. How does the per capita consumption of marijuana in the Netherlands compare to that of the United States?

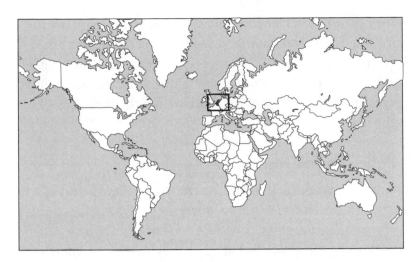

I was somewhere around [the canal] Oudezijds Voorburg-wal, on the edge of Amsterdam's Red Light District [neighborhood known for prostitution], when I knew that the drugs would never take hold. My vision was bad, but then it always is; my judgment was no worse than normal; and my usual bleak mood was no better. I had absolutely no interest in tie-dye, [German-Swiss writer] Hermann Hesse, granny glasses, world peace, the teachings of the Buddha, or a flower in my hair. I was a loser Leary [refers to theories of psychologist Timothy Leary], a deadbeat De Quincey [Thomas De Quincey was best known for his autobiographical 1822 book, *Confessions of an English Opium-Eater*].

"Cannabis is not exactly legal in the Netherlands. But it's not exactly illegal either. Finding out exactly what the country's policy of tolerance (gedoogbeleid) means is about as easy as following stoner logic."

It had all seemed so much simpler just a few hours before. I'd been sitting in an old café on Spuistraat [street in the center of Amsterdam] discussing the state of Dutch politics (bad) over a few Dutch beers (good) with my friend Henk. Sixteen *biertjes* [beers] later (between us, *between* us), it was time to move on. Henk was saying something feeble about a heavily pregnant wife, had to be by her side, baby due any moment, and I, well, I felt the call of investigative journalism. Holland's reefer [marijuana] madness had to be checked out. Thoroughly.

A Policy of Tolerance

Cannabis is not exactly legal in the Netherlands. But it's not exactly illegal either. Finding out exactly what the country's policy of tolerance (*gedoogbeleid*) means is about as easy as following stoner logic, but its result is that, in certain cities, so-called "coffee shops" are allowed to sell small amounts of cannabis (a maximum of five grams at a time) to their customers. Coffee shops are licensed; they pay tax and are regulated: Alcohol is rarely on offer, hard drugs are strictly forbidden, and even soft drugs cannot be advertised. No minors are permitted on the premises, and you have to be 18 before you can graze on the grass [marijuana] (the drinking age in the Netherlands is 16). Finally, in a last, faint, despairing echo of the country's Calvinist [religious doctrine of John Calvin] past, a coffee shop can be closed down if it's a "nuisance."

And in recent years, many have been. As always, when anything bad happens, France is involved. Concerned by the number of their nationals traveling to the Netherlands to stock up on pot, both France and Germany have been putting pressure on the Dutch to close down the coffee shops, or at least insist that only Dutch citizens be permitted to use them. For the most part, the Dutch have paid no attention, but the purchase limit was reduced to the current five grams (from thirty) and other regulations were more strictly enforced. According to the possibly reliable *Smokers Guide to Amsterdam* ("an unbiased view of Amsterdam for casual party people"), the number of coffee shops in the city fell from 480 in 1990 to 279 in 2001. Once the less permissive center-right Christian

Democrats came to power in 2002 this crackdown went further still. A little over 200 coffee shops survive there today [2005].

But that was more than enough to choose from. Even after I had, um, weeded out the coffee shops with names that were either too redolent of the 1960s (The Doors, Flower, Kasbah, the Kashmir Lounge, Mellow Yellow, and Pink Floyd), too scary (Lucifera, Ruthless, Stud, and Xtreme), too derivative (Rick's Café), too tactless (Midnight-Express), or unacceptably dependent on puns (High School, High Time, Highlander, and Highway), a wide selection still remained. Some were too seedy, others too hip; the place I eventually found was relaxed and welcoming even if some of the people there appeared really, *really* surprised to see me.

Perhaps my suit, tie, and shirt (Jermyn Street, since you ask) were to blame. Or was the problem my age, a [Tom] Cruise-[Katie] Holmes [actors] span [sixteen years] away from that of the pretty young waitress? Maybe it was just that I quite clearly didn't know what I was doing. I hadn't brought any tobacco with me, or any rolling papers, or even a lighter. The menu was meaningless, but vaguely alarming. White Widow? Bubblegum? Domina Haze? Manali Crema? I felt confident that AK47 was not the way to go, but as for the rest . . .

"Have you ever smoked?" asked the young, young, *young* waitress, anxiously.

"I was at university during the 1970s," I replied ambiguously, plagiarizing Newt Gingrich.

She laughed, and I bought five pre-rolled joints for twenty euros—dope for beginners, I suspected, a "trip" with training wheels. I smoked them quietly in a corner, reading *The Economist* (what did you expect, *High Times*?), while the other customers sat across the room, puffing on Bubblegum, occasionally glancing over at this misplaced Methuselah [extremely old man] and his *Economist* and wondering, probably, whether the BTK killer ["Bind, Torture, Kill" serial killer arrested in 2005] had been caught after all. After an hour or so, nothing seemed to be happening. The joints *smelled* like 1967, but their effect was 1957. Had years of legal intoxicants taken their toll, or had I simply been had? Supplementing my sad-sap spliffs [marijuana cigarettes] with more potent space cakes [cake made with marijuana] ("once you're on the ride," cautioned the *Smokers Guide*, "there's no immediate way off!") seemed unwise. It was time to go. So I did.

If space cakes were unwise, Amsterdam's "smart shops" look really dumb. These stoner apothecaries, a more recent arrival, sell not cannabis, but a wide selection of nature's naughtier productions: herbs, mushrooms, cacti, and odd, unidentifiable fungi of the type that usually means trouble in sci-fi movies too low-budget to spring for a proper alien. Some of their offerings may not work at all: To believe in a "natural Viagra best boiled in vodka" took, I felt, brains more thoroughly boiled in vodka even than mine. Others may work all too well: After some Salvia [psychoactive herb], "your balance is completely lost; gravity pulls you in amazing ways." Oh, okay.

An Uncertain Future for Amsterdam

But Holland as a whole has not lost its balance. There's no room to recite all the arguments here, but if the coffee-shop experiment has not worked quite as well as some of its boosters claim, its critics have fared even worse. Per capita cannabis consumption in the Netherlands is estimated to be at the EU [European Union] average, and rather below that prevailing in these Altered States of America; and the Dutch, of course, have avoided much of the destruction, despair, and cost of the drug wars. Disappointingly for drug warriors, there's no evidence either that easy access to cannabis has acted as a "gateway" to more dangerous pastimes: The incidence of heroin

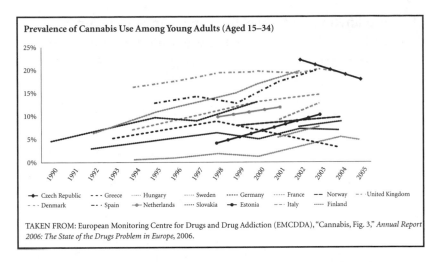

Prevalence of Cannabis Use Among Young Adults (Aged 15–34)

Czech Republic - - - Greece ····· Hungary ····· Sweden ····· Germany ····· France —— Norway - - - United Kingdom
- - - Denmark —·· Spain —●— Netherlands ····· Slovakia —●— Estonia —·· Italy ····· Finland

TAKEN FROM: European Monitoring Centre for Drugs and Drug Addiction (EMCDDA), "Cannabis, Fig. 3," *Annual Report 2006: The State of the Drugs Problem in Europe*, 2006.

consumption is far less than in the U.S. Overall, Holland has one of the lowest rates of problem drug use in Western Europe.

If there is an objection to the coffee shops, it's aesthetic. Owing to them, Amsterdam has become to cannabis what Bourbon Street [in New Orleans, Louisiana] is to Hurricanes. This fine old bourgeois city is in danger of turning into a euro-Kathmandu [capital of Nepal], a druggy destination overwhelmed by day trippers (literally), cannabis kitsch, and counterculture dreck [trash]—which could end up destroying the typically civil Dutch compromise that has made this experiment possible.

And then there are the town's proliferating cannabis snobs, like wine bores only, somehow, even more irritating. You can read what they have to say (Nepal Temple Balls have, apparently, a "buzzy, chatty high that makes you zone") on coffeeshop menus and in numerous guidebooks. Or go and hear for yourself. I joined the crowd downstairs at the "Cannabis College" on [the canal] Oudezijdes Achterburgwal to gaze at some outlaw botany and listen to the mumbling, muttering, meandering Yoda [a *Star Wars* character] who was its custodian. I could take the interminable, rambling discussion of the merits of one plant over another, but when he started referring to them as his "girls," I knew that it was time for something else: A good, stiff drink.

Canadians Are Unnecessarily Challenged in Obtaining Medical Marijuana

Connie Howard

In the following viewpoint, Connie Howard argues that Canada's medical marijuana program has been a complete failure. Too many obstacles are in place, she argues, making it nearly impossible for those in need to acquire a license for the drug. For those who do manage, they face an even greater challenge with supply and are currently limited to an inferior pharmaceutical version that is not potent enough to help alleviate their pain. In addition, the synthetic form also causes many side effects. A better program is needed, she maintains, and quality cannabis should be made readily available for those choosing to use marijuana as medicine. Howard pens the health column "Well, Well, Well" for the alternative newspaper Vue Weekly.

As you read, consider the following questions:

1. According to Howard, marijuana was prescribed freely by Canadian physicians until what year?
2. What is wrong with the cannabis being provided through Canada's authorized dealer Prairie Plant Systems (PPS), according to the author?
3. How is inhalation of the herbal form of marijuana better than the synthetic form, as argued by the author?

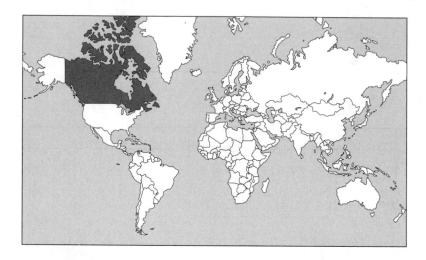

I need to chime in on the drug conversation, at least with respect to the only illegal drug I know anything about.

Recent news of the safety of marijuana relative to alcohol and tobacco is, of course, not really news. Nor is the truth that Health Canada's medical marijuana program has mostly failed those who wish to use marijuana as medicine.

Most of us know that our current government has no intention of resurrecting the Marijuana Reform Bill, which intended not to legalize possession but to decriminalize it and replace jail sentences for possession of small amounts with fines.

What might be news to many, however, is that marijuana was prescribed freely by Canadian physicians until full prohibition in 1932 (recreational use has been prohibited since 1923) and by traditional healers for thousands of years. Many experts say evidence of its therapeutic value is indisputable and users say it is more effective and has infinitely fewer negative effects than codeine as a pain reliever.

Help Is out of Reach for Those Most in Need

But the barriers one must overcome in pursuit of a licence for medical marijuana are high, high enough to be out of reach for many. Though the first one—a physician's signature—is technically not impossible for the seriously ill (those with multiple sclerosis, spinal cord injury, spinal cord disease, cancer, AIDS/HIV, severe arthritis and epilepsy), doctors don't sign readily.

And for those in the category that includes all other illness, getting a licence is a pipe dream—they need a declaration from a specialist who deems conventional pharmaceutical treatments for their problem are ineffective or medically inappropriate.

Those who find that marijuana alleviates their symptoms of depression or attention deficit or insomnia or fibromyalgia or panic might just as well not trouble themselves with the application process—we do, after all, have real medicines to deal with those things, things like Zoloft and Prozac and Valium and Ativan and Flurazepam and Ritalin and Adderall. All of which come with extensive tiny-print fast-talking risk warnings, of course, and all of which are making those in the pharmaceutical business very wealthy, but no matter.

The next hoop, for those few who do make it through the first one, is supply. Health Canada's authorized dealer, Prairie Plant Systems (PPS), provides only one strain of cannabis—a product those in the know say is inferior in every way. (It has been irradiated, is not grown organically, and isn't potent enough for medical use.)

Nonprofit compassion clubs serve thousands of chronically ill persons in Canada, providing access to clean, high quality cannabis; in exchange, they continue to risk arrest and criminal prosecution.

Health Canada has stated in court that compassion clubs have historically provided a safe source to those with medical need. But on the licence application there is no option to choose compassion clubs as a supply source. Applicants after a high quality legal product are out of luck. Hoops for those in need, loopholes for those in power.

Nonprofit compassion clubs serve thousands, though, providing access to a variety of strains of clean, high quality cannabis. And in exchange for their compassion for the chronically ill, they continue to risk arrest and criminal prosecution.

Verbal Form Not Patentable

Official favouring of pharmaceutical THC over natural health care practitioners who have experience with herbal medicine (which cannabis is) is no surprise. But, aside from the risks of smoke inhalation [Tetrahydrocannibinol Synthetic cannabis], which can be avoided with a vaporizer, the herb has definite advantages over the pharmaceutical version. Users of the synthetic form report more side effects, and absorption is slower and inconsistent. Inhalation of the herb is fast and provides flexible and exact dose control. It's just that the herbal form isn't patentable.

My own generation is definitely more wary of non-sanctioned medication than younger adults are—eyebrows tend to go up at the mention of marijuana. But these same adults, confident that our solidly trustworthy governments have our best interests in mind, think nothing of throwing ever-growing handfuls of sanctioned drugs into their poor unsuspecting bodies day after day, year after year, never stopping to ask how they'll ever get off the treadmill of managing symptoms and side-effects.

It's fine to care about the laws of the land, awkward and regressive as they sometimes are, but our laws—from the drugs they sanction and the resulting superbugs and side effects, to industry and farming and fast-food and neighbourhood lawn-care practices—are killing us.

Philosopher Ivan Illich claims for himself "the liberty to refuse any and all medical treatment at any time ... the liberty to take any drug or treatment of my own choosing; the liberty to be treated by the person of my choice ... whether that person be an acupuncturist, a homeopathic physician, [or] a neurosurgeon."

It sounds reasonable to me.

Bolivia's Criminalization of Coca Should Be Overturned

Danna Harman

In the following viewpoint, Danna Harman discusses Bolivian president Evo Morales's plans for decriminalizing coca in Bolivia. Harman emphasizes the Bolivians' use of the coca leaf within the local, legal market, and not as a drug. Harman also discusses how coca is turned into cocaine, and how some Bolivians are sustained by the cocaine business. Danna Harman serves as the Latin America correspondent for The Christian Science Monitor *and* USA Today.

As you read, consider the following questions:

1. According to the viewpoint, about how many acres of coca does Bolivia grow per year?
2. Over the centuries, how have the indigenous Bolivians used the coca leaf?
3. Who are the *cocaleros?*

Chimore, Bolivia—It is the day after Evo Morales's victory in Bolivia's elections, and the special forces counternarcotics teams are streaming back into their base in the Chapare jungle. Col. Rosalio Alvarez Claros, commander of the base,

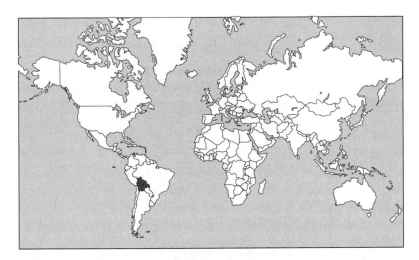

watches them from his office window. "We will continue with our work here, as usual, until someone tells us to stop," he says softly, ". . . and that hasn't happened yet."

But such an order might not be far off.

"Bolivia grows approximately 67,000 acres of coca a year. . . . Of those . . . 38,000 acres are cultivated legally and used for local consumption."

Decriminalizing Coca

Mr. Morales campaigned on the promise of decriminalizing coca. This is seen as a slap in the face to the US [United States], which gives Bolivia—the world's third-largest coca producer after Colombia and Peru—$150 million in aid every year, most of which goes toward the eradication of coca, the destruction of cocaine labs, and finding alternative agricultural projects.

Morales's stance on coca may also have regional ramifications. In neighboring Peru—the world's second-biggest coca-leaf provider, with more than 123,000 acres under cultivation—rising political star Ollanta Humala, a populist leader like Morales, has also vowed to decriminalize coca if elected president in April.

"There is as radical a coca movement here as in Bolivia, and the two coordinate," says Jaime Antesana Rivera, a narcotrafficking expert at Lima's Instituto Peruano de Economia y Politica (IPEP). "Morales's victory will certainly have an impact here, favoring the coca growers and further confounding US counternarcotics efforts in the whole region."

Bolivia grows approximately 67,000 acres of coca a year, according to Col. Luis Caballero Tirado, head of Bolivia's counternarcotics police force (FELCN). Of those, under an agreement with the Bolivian government, 38,000 acres are cultivated legally and used for local consumption.

Legal Coca vs. Illegal Cocaine

Revered for centuries by indigenous Bolivians, people use the coca leaf in ceremonies and chew it, saying that it wards off hunger and fights illness. Coca tea, meanwhile, is everywhere, sold in markets and served in tourist hotels.

The remainder of Bolivia's coca is grown illegally and turned into cocaine, says Caballero. The US State Department estimates that Bolivia produces and sends 71 tons of cocaine to the world market a year.

Drug statistics are often conflicting, or vague. Different reports out of the State Department itself estimate that, overall, anywhere between 358 and 744 tons of cocaine came into the US alone last year. A full 90 percent of that amount comes from Colombia, the region's biggest producer by far. Most of the $6 billion the US has spent on fighting drugs since 2000 has also gone to Colombia, a close US ally.

"We are sustained by coca," says Leandro Valencia, a *cocalero*, or coca grower, who admits his plots are illegal. "I put my three children through school on coca money. . . . My daughter even learned how to drive [with proceeds].... You talk about drug problems, but whose problem is that? I care about money for my family."

The Coca Leaf of Cocaine Paste Process

Two-and-a-half acres of coca produces about 750 to 1,000 kilos (1,650 to 2,200 lbs.) of coca leaf a year, explains Caballero. This coca leaf is typically sold to middle men who take it to makeshift outdoor jungle laboratories nearby, where it is mashed and processed into a chunky cocaine paste.

That paste is moved out of the region to more sophisticated labs where it is refined. It is then transported out of Bolivia, hidden in everything from human stomachs to TV sets.

Some of the Bolivian cocaine goes to the US, but most, says Caballero, moves through Brazil to Europe. Local cocaine use has gone up 200 percent in the past decade, says the colonel.

The *cocaleros* here are paid anywhere between $800 and $1,000 for providing the coca leaves for one kilo of cocaine paste.

Once processed, the price of that kilo of paste cocaine goes up to $2,500, according to Caballero. Out on the streets of the US, that same kilo will have been diluted and become two or three kilos of the drug and be sold for anywhere between $220,000 and $240,000.

Growing coca, says Valencia, he can make "ten times" what he would make by growing pineapples or yucca, a staple crop here—and he does not have to worry about transportation to market, or buyers. It is estimated about 1,500 extended families in Chapare live off the cocaine business.

Catching Narcotraffickers

In 2005, Bolivian military units uprooted and destroyed 19,800 acres of coca fields, while the US Drug Enforcement Administration-trained FELCN destroyed 3,888 jungle cocaine

Fallout from Coca Laws

For many Bolivians, U.S. intervention in Bolivia has left a distinctly bitter taste. Bolivia's draconian drug control law, Ley 1008, implemented in 1988 under heavy U.S. pressure, made illegal any coca cultivation beyond a 12,000-hectare limit specified as sufficient for meeting legal demand. The law also criminalized many campesino coca growers by not discriminating between cocaine and the unprocessed coca leaf. In 2004, 40 percent of people in Bolivia's jails were imprisoned under Ley 1008, and 77 percent of them remained uncharged with any crime, this even after a 1999 reform.

Gretchen Gordon,
"The United States, Bolivia and the Political Economy of Coca,"
Multinational Monitor, *January–February 2006.*

labs, confiscated almost 50 tons of cocaine paste, and arrested 4,208 narcotraffickers, according to official statistics.

"[Evo] Morales does not intend to be soft on narcotrafficking: 'Yes to coca, no to cocaine,' is his motto."

"We catch more—they produce more—then we catch more," says Alvarez. "The narcotraffickers have more money and better technology than we do. So, who's winning? It is hard to say."

Morales stresses that he does not intend to be soft on narcotrafficking: "Yes to coca, no to cocaine," is his motto. He has repeatedly suggested that the additional coca cultivated would be absorbed by the local, legal market, or alternatively would jump-start a legal coca export industry with coca tea, coca wine, soft drinks, and coca toothpaste. But details on these plans remain sketchy.

The special forces teams have been out since dawn, between them walking hundreds of miles. They return drenched in sweat and with little to show for their efforts. The day's tally: one lab destroyed, and one vehicle carrying 15 kilos of sulfuric acid and 200 kilos of coca leaf stopped on the region's lone two-lane highway.

It's not much, admits agent Dennis Escobar Revollo, but, he explains: "It seems everyone was busy celebrating Evo's victory." The narcotraffickers know, he adds ruefully ". . .that they will have plenty of time for cocaine later."

Periodical Bibliography

The following articles have been selected to supplement the diverse views presented in this chapter.

Drug Policy Alliance Network	"Alternatives to Prohibition," 2008. www.drug policy.org.
Drug War Facts	"The Netherlands and the United States: A Comparison," May 29, 2007. www.drugwar facts.org.
Richard Ford	"Cannabis Goes Back to Class B Despite Drug Experts' Verdict," *The Times* (London), May 8, 2008. www.timesonline.co.uk.
Lawrence O. Gostin	"Medical Marijuana, American Federalism, and the Supreme Court," *JAMA*, vol. 294, no. 7, August 17, 2005, pp. 842–844.
Gary Greenberg	"Respectable Reefer," *Mother Jones*, November/December 2005. www.motherjones.com.
Caitlin Hughes and Alex Stevens	"The Effects of Decriminalization of Drugs in Portugal," The Beckley Foundation, December 1, 2007.
Simon Lenton	"Pot, Politics and the Press: Reflections on Cannabis Law Reform in Western Australia," *Drug and Alcohol Review*, vol. 23, no. 2, June 2004, pp. 223–233.
Antonia Leslie	"The War Isn't Working So Is It Now Time to Consider the Unthinkable and Legalise All Drugs?" *Irish Independent* (UK), September 3, 2006.
Christopher Scanlon	"Zero-Tolerance Drug Policies Too Easily Abandon the User," *The Age*, May 23, 2007. www.theage.com.au.
Norm Stamper	"Leave the Dopers Alone," AlterNet, October 20, 2005. www.alternet.org.

GLOBAL VIEWPOINTS

CHAPTER 5

Fighting Drugs Through Harm Reduction Strategies

Harm Reduction Reduces Drug Use and Restores Human Dignity

Drug Policy Alliance

As the war on drugs has consistently failed to curb the steady flow of illicit drugs, many countries have decided to turn away from prohibition and focus their efforts instead upon harm reduction. Supporters of this strategy believe that in reducing the harms associated with drug use and providing assistance and rehabilitation to addicts, drug abuse will decrease—and so too will trafficking and its associated crimes. Harm reduction can be observed today through needle-exchange programs, assisted injection centers, and heroin maintenance programs. The following viewpoint explains the methodology behind this strategy and addresses the far-reaching benefits that can be realized.

As you read, consider the following questions:

1. While current policies gauge changes in drug use rates, how is the success of a harm reduction strategy measured?

2. How is incarceration counterproductive as a drug control policy?

3. What are some of the societal harms resulting from an overemphasis on prohibition?

Harm reduction is a public health philosophy that seeks to lessen the dangers that drug abuse and our drug policies cause to society. A harm reduction strategy is a comprehensive approach to drug abuse and drug policy. Harm reduction's complexity lends to its misperception as a drug legalization tool.

Reducing Harm: Treatment and Beyond

Harm reduction rests on several basic assumptions. A basic tenet of harm reduction is that there has never been, is not now, and never will be a drug-free society.

A harm reduction strategy seeks pragmatic solutions to the harms that drugs and drug policies cause. It has been said that harm reduction is not what's nice, it's what works.

A harm reduction approach acknowledges that there is no ultimate solution to the problem of drugs in a free society, and that many different interventions may work. Those interventions should be based on science, compassion, health and human rights.

"A harm reduction approach advocates lessening the harms of drugs through education, prevention, and treatment."

A harm reduction strategy demands new outcome measurements. Whereas the success of current drug policies is primarily measured by the change in use rates, the success of a harm reduction strategy is measured by the change in rates of death, disease, crime and suffering.

Because incarceration does little to reduce the harms that ever-present drugs cause to our society, a harm reduction approach favors treatment of drug addiction by health care professionals over incarceration in the penal system.

AIDS Crisis Brings Radical Change in Iran's Response to Heroin Use

Fearing an AIDS epidemic, Iran's theocratic government has dropped a zero-tolerance policy against increasingly common heroin use and now offers addicts low-cost needles, methadone and a measure of social acceptance.

For two decades, Iran largely avoided the global AIDS crisis. But today, officials are alarmed by a 25 percent HIV infection rate that one survey has found among hard-core heroin users and worry that addicts may channel the virus into the population of 68 million.

Supporters of the government's new approach laud it as practical and devoid of the wishful thinking and moralism that they contend hampers policies on drug abuse and AIDS in some other countries, including the United States. "I have to pay tribute to Iran on this," said Roberto Arbitrio, head of the U.N. [United Nations] Office on Drugs and Crime in Tehran.

Bijan Nasirimanesh, who heads a drop-in clinic that dispenses needles, bleach and methadone in a hard-hit area of south Tehran, said, "It's ironic that Iran, very fundamentalist, very religious—very religious—has been able to convince itself" to embrace such policies.

Karl Vick,
"AIDS Crisis Brings Radical Change in Iran's
Response to Heroin Use," The Washington Post, *July 5, 2005.*

Because some drugs, such as marijuana, have proven medicinal uses, a harm reduction strategy not only seeks to reduce the harm that drugs cause, but also to maximize their potential benefits.

A harm reduction strategy recognizes that some drugs, such as marijuana, are less harmful than others, such as cocaine and alcohol. Harm reduction mandates that the emphasis on intervention should be based on the relative harmfulness of the drug to society.

A harm reduction approach advocates lessening the harms of drugs through education, prevention, and treatment.

Harm reduction seeks to reduce the harms of drug policies dependent on an overemphasis on interdiction, such as arrest, incarceration, establishment of a felony record, lack of treatment, lack of adequate information about drugs, the expansion of military source control intervention efforts in other countries, and intrusion on personal freedoms.

Harm reduction also seeks to reduce the harms caused by an overemphasis on prohibition, such as increased purity, black market adulterants, black market sale to minors, and black market crime.

A harm reduction strategy seeks to protect youth from the dangers of drugs by offering factual, science-based drug education and eliminating youth's black market exposure to drugs.

Finally, harm reduction seeks to restore basic human dignity to dealing with the disease of addiction.

Harm Reduction Encourages Drug Use and Is Dehumanizing

Theodore Dalrymple

In the following viewpoint, Theodore Dalrymple makes a case against harm reduction. He argues that it displaces responsibility for the addict, instead making authority figures accountable for the negative outcomes of the addict's own self-destructive behavior. Anthony Daniels, who uses the pen name "Theodore Dalrymple," is a retired doctor who spent most of his career working as a hospital and prison physician. In addition to authoring several books, Dalrymple has written regularly for the London Spectator *and* National Review *for many years.*

As you read, consider the following questions:

1. What happens when consequences are removed from dangerous self-indulgent actions, according to Dalrymple?
2. Why is harm reduction an infantilizing policy?
3. According to the author, what typically happens in cases of "prison retoxification," as addicts celebrate their release with drugs?

The object of treatment, so called, is either the abstention [self-denial] of the addicted person, or if that proves to be "impossible" (I use the word metaphorically), harm reduction. This means that if a person insists upon taking heroin by intravenous injection, you provide him with the needles and syringes so that he should not suffer the transmissible diseases from needles and syringes used by other addicts. (In Canadian prison recently, the authorities have offered to provide prisoners with tattoos to prevent them from tattooing themselves, a procedure that involves risk. They must, however, choose non-racist, non-violent designs.) This policy certainly seems to reduce the chances of an addict contracting HIV or hepatitis B and C. If a person persists in taking opiates, and in committing crime to obtain the money to pay for them, you provide him with free opiates so that he commits no more crime. And so on and so forth, always in the direction of accommodation of the habit, of course.

The addict is not to be confronted directly with the consequences of his own actions; in modern society, we want our risk and our safety too. It is the modern equivalent of eating one's cake and having it.

The benefits of what is called risk-reduction are tangible, or at least measurable. The benefits of refusing to reduce risk are intangible or philosophical, though it is possible in the long run that they would translate into tangible, or measurable, ones. When self-indulgent actions, such as taking heroin, are deprived of some their worst consequences, it is hardly to be wondered at that they spread like wildfire through a population. If consequences are removed from enough actions, then the very concept of human agency evaporates, life itself becomes meaningless, and is thenceforth a vacuum in which people oscillate between boredom and oblivion. They have nothing to hope for and nothing to fear; they are more likely to seek the intermittent oblivion of opiate addiction.

Facing Responsibilities

Harm reduction as a policy is inherently infantilizing of the population: it assumes that the authorities are, and ought to be, responsible, for the ill-consequences of what people insist upon doing. A recent case in a Canadian women's prison illustrates this. A prisoner, addicted to opiates, was given a dose of methadone to prevent her from suffering; but so slight was the suffering that she anticipated, no doubt from her previous experience, from withdrawal from opiates—the suffering that supposedly justified the prescription in the first place—that she voluntarily vomited up her methadone, to give it, or more likely to sell it, to another prisoner who was not an addict. The latter drank the former's vomit, and died as a consequence.

Harm reduction is an infantilizing policy, treating users as if they are not responsible for their own actions.

Who was to blame? The prison authorities, of course. The relatives of the deceased immediately sued them. There is thus no reasonable expectation that people should not drink one another's vomitus, or that, if they do, they should take the consequences themselves. We are all children, and the authorities are our parents.

This is utilitarianism made policy. It infantilizes the subject, however, and treats him as if he were not responsible for his own actions. In fact, experience shows that the subject is not quite such an automaton as is often made out (a subject to which I shall return): for example, in the prison in which I work, the vast majority of heroin addicts who inject themselves with the drug give up injecting because clean needles are not made available to them, and they are aware of the dangers of injecting with needles that others have already used. This suggests that, at the very least, prisoners are conscious, and indeed self-conscious, beings. Of course, a small number of such addicts continue to inject, putting themselves at risk, and it is this small minority upon whom policy makers, always biased in favour of more official intervention, focus their attention. There is nothing an official hates more than a person who makes up his own mind.

The Policy of Retoxification

My experience is not unique. It has been found in formal surveys in Scotland, for example, that the majority of injecting addicts do not inject once they are in prison. They know what they are doing. Nevertheless, it is up to the authorities to prevent prisoners from starting to take drugs in prison. A paper in the *British Medical Journal* stated that "Prisons need to understand how initiation [into injecting] occurs and to support non-injectors . . . so that they can avoid starting to inject inside." The very language of this paper turns those who choose to inject heroin in prison for the first time into billiard balls impacted upon by other billiard balls.

The *ne plus ultra* [pinnacle, highest point] of the harm-reduction philosophy, however, is to be found in the policy of retoxification introduced in some Scottish prisons. Addicts who stop taking heroin in prison sometimes celebrate their release—within hours, not days—by taking an injection of heroin. As they have lost their physiological tolerance to the drug in the meantime, and as they often take the dose to which they were accustomed before they were sent to prison, quite a number of them die. Others end up in intensive care units of local hospitals, where their lives are saved.

It is not always or even usually a lack of knowledge about the facts of tolerance that leads them to this dangerous behavior. I recall a prisoner who was a heroin addict and who was due for release in the near future, whom I warned of the dangers of reduced tolerance. The day following his release, I met him again in the hospital in which I also work, and which is

Canadian Needle Exchange Program Under Fire

This syringe's life begins at a downtown needle exchange program.

It's picked up by a female addict.

She's already got her crack cocaine and, along with a few other addicts, leaves with the needle.

They take it to a city parking garage. . . .

The crack is cooked with city-issued materials. The needle sucks in the drug. It pricks the arm of one. Then the foot of another.

The needle is used by three addicts, including her. . . .

It's all over in about 10 minutes and the needle is left on the ground.

Its fate is shared by thousands of needles each year. . . .

The city began handing out clean syringes in 1991 when Ottawa Public Health implemented the needle exchange program. . . .

The [program] gives addicts sterile needles in the hope of getting dirty ones back in return.

According to the city's Web site, however, "no client will be refused sterile needles on the basis that they do not have any used needles to exchange."

The program has come under fire by several city councillors who have demanded a review. . . .

Councillors want a detailed report to help the city increase the effectiveness of the harm-reduction program.

Their ultimate goal is a one-for-one exchange.

Kenneth Jackson, "The Life of an Addict,"
Ottawa Sun, April 12, 2008.

next door to the prison; he had taken heroin and had briefly needed artificial ventilation as a result.

"Did you remember what I told you?" I asked.

"Yes."

"Didn't you believe me?"

"Yes, I believed you."

"Then why did you take no notice?"

"I met up with my old friends."

The anticipated pleasure was great, the price was right, and the temptation strong. All of us know what it is like to give in to temptation, and to that extent the man was deserving of our compassion. It was right to save his life, but would it have been right to tell him that he had done no wrong, or that like [theologian Martin] Luther he could have done no other? Would not that have been to turn him into something less than a man?

This is what the prison retoxification scheme seeks to do. Recognizing that some prisoners like the one I have just described are inclined to die as a result of their celebratory heroin injection (indeed, their death rate in the two weeks following release from prison may be thirty-four times as high as at any other time outside prison), their tolerance to opiates is deliberately increased in prison after a period of abstinence so that they may safely inject on their release. Thus their decision to inject themselves is treated like a natural fact that is independent of human volition, which is to say that they are not like you and me, who for good or ill make up our own minds about what to do and suffer the consequences. They are mere objects, to be manipulated in a technocratic fashion, to be given drugs as a machine is oiled, so that it won't seize up; and while this is dehumanizing, and puts them in a humiliating position *vis-à-vis* [facing] their would-be benefactors, it also gives them a certain weak-minded gratification of the kind to which they have already proved themselves susceptible. A vicious circle of mutual pretense between benefactor and recipient is set up. . . . Meanwhile, the fact that the overall death rate of addicts during the time they are sent to prison plus the two weeks after their release is not greater than an equivalent period outside prison altogether suggests that imprisonment without release exerts a life-preserving effect upon them. It is their release into freedom that kills them, not their imprisonment; a sad commentary upon their lives no doubt, but one whose philosophical, ethical, and practical significance entirely escapes the harm-avoidance drug treatment school of thought.

Canada's Safe-Injection Program Is Curtailing Abuse and Saving Lives

Mark Follman

In the following viewpoint, Mark Follman investigates how the first experimental safe injection site in North America has helped to change a Vancouver community and save hundreds of lives. A case of harm reduction in action, supporters are seeing many benefits of this program; it treats addicts as patients but helps to reinstate their dignity. Rather than having to use drugs alone in the streets—sharing needles and risking an overdose—the supervised injection site has provided a safe haven where users can receive intervention, and most importantly, rehabilitation. Mark Follman is deputy news editor for Salon.com

As you read, consider the following questions:

1. In addition to preventing overdose emergencies, what other kinds of medical interventions does the safe injection site perform on a regular basis?

2. According to Follman, what were some of the fears conservative opponents had regarding the safe injection site?

3. While mirrors inside the injection booths are there to help the clinical staff watch users, what other purpose have they served?

Mark Follman, "The Needle and the Damage Undone," Salon.com, September 22, 2006. This article first appeared in Salon.com, at www.salon.com. An online version remains in the Salon archives. Reprinted with permission.

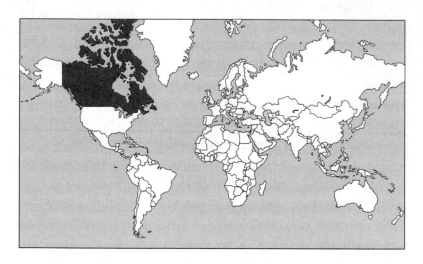

Three years ago [in 2002], Vancouver opened a bold new front in the eternal war on drugs. In a downtown neighborhood notorious for street addicts, health care workers began welcoming clients into a new "safe injection site," a legal facility for users of illegal narcotics such as heroin and cocaine.

"The Insite program has saved hundreds of lives. It has wiped away much of the drug use in the surrounding streets."

Since then, 18 hours a day, seven days a week, users have been free to enter Insite, located in a renovated storefront at 135 East Hastings Street, and inject their own drugs under the supervision of health care professionals. Inside, there are 12 individual booths where users shoot up. They are given clean gear, including needles, spoons and tourniquets. Afterward, they are free to relax in an adjacent "chill-out" room, where they can drink coffee and watch TV. They can also get medical advice and information about rehabilitation programs.

The operation, which today remains the only one of its kind in North America, is funded and run by the provincial

Canadian government. This month, the federal government was set to rule on whether to extend Insite's legal status, but has decided to delay the decision [until June 30, 2008]. In the meantime, Insite will be allowed to continue operating while additional studies are conducted into how the program affects treatment, prevention and crime.

For drug experts across North America, it will continue to be a closely watched experiment in curtailing drug use, and related crime and urban blight. They know that eradicating the world's supply of illicit narcotics is a statistical impossibility. According to the United Nations' 2006 World Drug Report, despite a record seizure of massive quantities of opiates—120 metric tons worldwide—law enforcement managed to intercept less than one-quarter of the total produced.

But while the war can never be won, Vancouver is winning a key battle. The Insite program has saved hundreds of lives. It has wiped away much of the drug use in the surrounding streets, while increasing the number of addicts seeking treatment and rehabilitation. Some local conservatives, once fierce opponents of the injection site, are now backing it. And supporters believe the site's success will prove a beachhead [secure position] for a less punitive and more humane war on drugs extending across Canada—even to drug-troubled cities south of the Canadian border.

By the time Insite opened in September 2003, Vancouver was reeling from a decade-long drug crisis, with an estimated 12,000 addicts in the city. That August, I spent some time in the bleak environs of the Downtown Eastside, home to one of the most desperate populations of junkies anywhere. The streets were littered with discarded needles and trash. They were also littered with bodies—nearly three per week on average, the victims of overdoses. Infectious disease ravaged the thousands of addicts in the neighborhood, some of whom dissolved their stashes using puddle water, or even their own blood, before fixing with shared needles in the back alleys. A third had contracted HIV, and no less than nine out of 10 were infected with hepatitis C. The situation had become so grim that authorities had tacitly allowed the operation of an illegal safe injection site run by neighborhood activists, while plans for the government's own, first set in motion in 1997, crawled forward.

On a warm day in late August this year, the same neighborhood felt strikingly different. While there were still plenty of indigent people around, the streets were cleaner, and the visceral sense of foreboding and despair was gone. On the sidewalk in front of Insite, flanked by a pornography store and a Chinese barber shop with bars on the windows, I met Nathan Allen, a bespectacled 29-year-old resident of the neighborhood. . . . helping run a community campaign to secure Insite's future. "Just seeing the renewed optimism of the neighborhood has been amazing," he told me. "It's been a dramatic change over the last three years. I remember a person dying almost every day out here. . . ."

Those victims and neighbors were a range of people, many of whom fit the image of a typical street junkie—homeless, broke and frail—and others who did not. Dean Wilson, a wiry middle-aged addict and neighborhood activist I met then, expressed the outrage many felt at the time about the glacial pace of the government's response to the crisis. "Our friends are out on the streets dying," he'd told me. "We'll do what we have to do, with or without the authorities." Wilson and the activist group Vancouver Area Network of Drug Users patrolled the back alleys for medical emergencies, handing out clean needles and guiding junkies to the illegal safe injection site, which was located in a decrepit storefront just a couple blocks from where Insite now operates.

The population they were urgently trying to save included hundreds of impoverished Canadian Aboriginals, and thousands of women, many of them sex workers. But there were also young professionals and college kids buying and using.

One of them, a student named Aaron, wearing a hooded sweatshirt and a backpack, had sat down next to me on a park bench at 1 a.m. He was soft-spoken, intelligent and articulate. He talked candidly of his failure to stay sober, and told of the city's then more aggressive law-enforcement approach to addicts. During a crackdown that April, "tons of cops were just jacking anybody on the street and throwing them into paddy wagons," he said. "It was like a war zone down here."

Nevertheless, disease kept spreading, and street junkies kept dropping.

"Shortly after Insite gained Canadian federal approval, President Bush's drug czar, John P. Walters, slammed the program as immoral . . . calling Vancouver's policy 'a lie' and 'state-sponsored personal suicide.'"

By June 2003, facing down the hostility of Canadian conservatives and [President George] Bush officials in Washington, the provincial Vancouver Coastal Health authority received an exemption under Canada's Controlled Drugs and Substances Act to establish and operate Insite for three years. It was approved as a pilot project to halt the devastation, with the additional goal of gleaning data useful to public policy makers. The British Columbia Ministry of Health put up $1.2 million (Canadian) to renovate the former retail space, and has supplied approximately $2 million annually for operating costs. Modeled after successful "harm-reduction" programs in Europe begun in the 1980s, the plan to open Insite had wide political support in a city socially progressive by most measures. It was part of then Mayor Larry Campbell's "four-pillars" strategy that also emphasized prevention, treatment and law enforcement—the latter targeting drug dealers, but not users, who were viewed as sick people in need of help rather than handcuffs.

Rising support for the policy north of the border agitated Washington. Shortly after Insite gained Canadian federal approval, President Bush's drug czar, John P. Walters, slammed the program as immoral. "There are no safe injection sites," he declared, calling Vancouver's policy "a lie" and "state-sponsored personal suicide."

Since Insite opened, there has not been a single death inside or connected to the facility among the more than 7,200 individuals who have used it—including at least 453 people who have overdosed. Preventing overdoses from ending in fatalities is a primary objective of the program. "Those were all overdose events that could have been life-threatening without immediate medical intervention," said Jeff West, a coordinator for Vancouver Coastal Health who has been on staff at Insite since its launch. "These are people who stop breathing, or who suffer seizures or aneurysms. If they pass out in an alley and nobody sees them, they are at risk of death."

From a public-health perspective, Vancouver's policy stands as a courageous risk and an unmistakable success. While 453 overdose emergencies averted is the official number cited in peer-reviewed studies of the program, there have been closer to 1,000 people in serious physical jeopardy who have been saved by Insite, according to West. "We also do a lot of other medical interventions," he said. "We see serious infections of organs and bones, lots of abscesses and skin wounds. The other day a nurse here treated a patient with a skin wound neglected for so long there were maggots in it." Such patients often have mental health issues as well. "A lot of people coming here are marginalized street addicts who wouldn't otherwise seek health care. Some of them are basically at death's door."

The injection site has been subject to rigorous, independent evaluation by the B.C. Centre for Excellence in HIV/ AIDS, a world-renowned research organization. For the period of the legal exemption, the federal government has funded the

Evidence of Safe Injection Site Success

Before Insite, many heroin addicts. . . . only had unsafe places to use while getting robbed, beaten up, arrested for the hit in their possession; they were sharing needles and using other unsanitary equipment. . . .

I helped manage Insite the first year it was open, so I saw the impact on the front line. Since then I have crossed paths with many addicts whose use of drugs and lives have stabilized to a much more functional, less street-involved existence.

Tanya Fader, "Insite: Safe Injection Site Fights for Life,"
Orato, *November 8, 2007. www.orato.com.*

Centre's research with a half-million dollars annually. Its findings, drawn from a two-year period ending in March 2006, have appeared in an array of leading publications, from the *Canadian Medical Association Journal* to the *New England Journal of Medicine* to the *Lancet*.

Insite has made a powerful impact on the drug crisis, beyond the lives saved. The sharing of needles among junkies . . . dropped 70 percent. Counsel available from professionals inside the facility has increased entry into detoxification programs and addiction treatment, with more than 4,000 referrals made, and one in five regular visitors beginning a detox program.

At the same time, fears initially raised by conservative opponents have not been realized. According to the research, the injection site has not led to an increased rate of relapse among former addicts. Nor has it proven a negative influence on those seeking to stop using, or resulted in a "honeypot effect"—the supposition that a free, government-sanctioned drug den would attract a swarm of users from beyond Vancouver.

And far fewer people are shooting up in public. "It used to churn my stomach—you would see four or five people lined up right there along the wall, injecting," Allen told me, pointing up the block to the Carnegie Community Center, a 100-year-old stone building whose grandeur was obscured by the street hustle. Centered on the corner of Main and Hastings, the drug scene has long been known as "pain and wasting." But while there is still a throng of addicts around, almost all injection drug use in the immediate area now takes place behind Insite's doors.

It's anything but a scene inside. The front reception area is clean and spare, with finished wood floors, contemporary light fixtures and a few chairs in a waiting area. It felt a universe apart from the shabby storefront that housed the illegal site at nearby 327 Carrall Street three years ago. (That site closed down a few months after Insite opened.) The day I visited, I was greeted by a friendly volunteer behind the desk, one of several user "peers" who help staff a government operation that might otherwise scare off street junkies.

"There's nothing glamorous or rock 'n' roll about using here. . . . You're cared for as a sick patient."

Dealing on the premises is strictly forbidden. The users share in "a culture of responsibility," according to West—they understand that the program's benefits, and its future, depend on upholding the government-mandated rules, and they help by reporting any wrongdoing to the staff.

"There's nothing glamorous or rock 'n' roll about using here," Allen noted, as we talked out front. "You're cared for as a sick patient." He also described one fortuitous side effect. The site's 12 injection booths are outfitted with mirrors to help the clinical staff keep watch over users—but they've also been a catalyst for vital self-reflection. "I've talked to several users who've told me that when they saw themselves in the mirror shooting up it really shook them," Allen said. "There was a moment of realization that couldn't have happened on the street. And now those people are in treatment, or they're clean."

Halfway up the block, a weathered-looking addict with stringy hair named Dan, on his way to fix, told me he felt In-site was "a lot safer" than using on the streets. For one thing, he said, "you don't have to worry about bad rigs no more." Initially he'd been wary of talking with a journalist. Two po-lice cars parked within 20 yards of us, however, did not ap-pear to bother him.

The Vancouver police department is among several agen-cies partnered in the city's harm-reduction strategy. That's led to some intriguing circumstances, given that Insite's users pur-chase and possess illegal substances, often nearby. Directly across the street from where I spoke with Dan, in an open al-ley behind the Carnegie Center, I observed two drug sales go down in less than 15 minutes. A parked patrol car sat across the street, directly facing the alley.

I approached the car and asked the young officer with close-cropped hair sitting behind the wheel about the dealing that had just taken place in plain sight of his car. Given the city's effort to decriminalize users, did officers sometimes look the other way? He agreed to speak to me only if he was not identified. "I guess you see what you see," he said. I mentioned how different the area appeared to be since my prior visit, which elicited a sliver of a polite smile. "It's a lot better out here now," he said.

"I think the police often feel like they're shoveling water in terms of street-level dealers," said West, the Insite coordinator. He suggested the police were more interested in focusing on bigger drug traffickers operating in the city. In the neighborhood around Main and Hastings, more critical to the police department's role in the harm-reduction strategy is maintaining public order and safety. "They're really quite supportive of the site," West added. "They know it's another tool that helps them do their job."

"If somebody's dealing drugs right in front of an officer, I can assure you they'd be dealt with," said Constable Howard Chow, speaking by phone from the public affairs office of the Vancouver P.D. He noted that the squad assigned to the Downtown Eastside, one of the city's most volatile sectors, regularly conducts surveillance and sweeps to bust dealers. But he acknowledged there were priorities. "Is simple possession as harshly looked upon as trafficking, for example? No. Those officers are often inundated with calls down there. We use the resources where they're most needed." He added, "We support the site in terms of the medical research, and helping see that through for its potential benefits. We don't comment on the right or wrong of it—that's not up to us."

The research on Insite also shows that it has not led to an increase in assaults, robberies or other drug-related crime— another fear that was played up by conservatives. Rates of vehicle break-ins and theft in the neighborhood "declined significantly," the research found. (When I visited in 2003, it was a big enough problem that one addict offered to keep watch over my car for me.) Still, according to West, there is a patrol car within a block at most hours of the night and day. The beat cops aren't just there for Insite—the immediate neighborhood keeps them busy in numerous ways, according to Chow—but without them, Insite would be more vulnerable to criminal drug activity and violence on or near the premises. In this respect, conservative critics say that securing a safe injection site with police resources is an additional cost to taxpayers in the tens of thousands of dollars.

Yet supporters of the program say the costs are more than made up for in the savings to the health care system. "The site encourages people to pay more attention to their own health issues—more of them get regular doctors rather than just using the emergency wards when their problems become acute," said West. "We know from area hospitals that it has relieved the burden significantly on local emergency rooms." The long view looks the same. As Fiona Gold, a nurse with the B.C. Center for Disease Control, told me in 2003, every HIV-infected addict dropped into the health care system costs the Canadian government an average of $150,000 in long-term care. The cost of a dozen such patients would cover Insite's operating expenses for a year.

There are other, less tangible considerations that can stand in the way of opening a safe injection site. "Plenty of people are going to feel like it sends the wrong message about a neighborhood," said Mark Kleiman, a former policy director in the U.S. Department of Justice who now heads the Drug Policy Analysis Program at UCLA. "Would you want one of these next door to you?"

Still, Kleiman says the potential benefits are undeniable. "Nobody's going to start using heroin because you've opened a safe injection site. Assuming you can keep crime in control, I don't see much downside," he said. "But there is a big upside in terms of public health and public order—I'm not surprised this has worked well in Vancouver. So is it a good idea for us to try this? Certainly."

There are certainly some U.S. cities in need of solutions, including in Washington's own backyard. Since the early 1990s, Baltimore has faced a drug crisis marked by rampant crime, the spread of HIV and hundreds of overdose deaths per year. (Indeed, HBO's gritty hit drama *The Wire*, which orbits around Baltimore's drug-plagued housing projects, is all too real.) According to Baltimore Health Commissioner Josh Sharfstein, authorities there believe the city is home to at least 40,000 heroin addicts—more than three times the number in Vancouver. Data from the Centers for Disease Control shows that thousands of them have contracted HIV through injection drug use.

Amid hot debate in 1994, Baltimore implemented a needle-exchange program, along with free condom distribution and medical screening services, to stop the spread of disease. Over the following decade that helped cut HIV transmission among users by 20 percent. Activists and advocacy groups in other urban drug centers such as New York, Chicago and San Francisco have for years experimented with harm-reduction measures at the grassroots level. But unlike Europe, and now Canada, the U.S. has never seen political will at the national level to help introduce harm-reduction measures—let alone a sanctioned injection site—to deal with the nation's hundreds of thousands of heroin addicts or other abundant populations of hard-drug abusers.

The Bush administration has often spoken of a "compassionate conservative" approach to social crises, but has emphasized only so-called faith-based and abstinence programs. Might they look at the results in Vancouver and consider exemption from federal drug laws for city governments under siege from drug-related disease and urban blight?

"Don't be ridiculous," Kleiman said flatly. "They're completely unserious about drug policy. It's an issue that's all about liberal-bashing to them, and playing to their base. I haven't seen them do anything counter to their own prejudices just because the science says they should."

Despite multiple calls seeking comment on Insite's results and legal status, Walters and the White House Office of National Drug Control Policy did not provide any response.

Over the past three years, Insite has built a compelling case for more places of its kind, say a range of advocates. As plans to launch it were gaining momentum in 2002, local leader George Chow was one of the program's most vocal opponents. President of the city's Chinese Benevolent Association and now a Vancouver city councilor, Chow ran as an independent that year, campaigning against the safe injection site and winning a seat on the council with strong support from the Chinese community. Chow had grown up in the Downtown Eastside, which includes the Chinatown district, and he shared the fears that many Chinatown merchants had about the harm-reduction plan.

That's all since changed. "It was a fear of the unknown—people were afraid such a facility would bring in more chaos," Chow said, speaking by phone from his office at City Hall. "After three years that has not happened, even with an increase in the homeless. Without this facility the drug problem would have been far more out of control. There would be an even bigger problem with HIV transmission and other issues."

Chow spoke with measured but unambiguous praise of the program. Insite has had a huge impact on the neighborhood, he said, though it certainly hasn't solved all its problems. "There is no easy solution," he said. "I think a lot of people still look at this as a moral issue, and it's challenging—but as a councilor, I believe we have to do all we can to deal with these health and social issues. This is most important, to work toward practical solutions."

And what of other drug hubs such as Toronto and Montreal? "I would advocate for a national plan, with more facilities like this in other cities," Chow said. "Not just an injection site, but also including treatment and education programs. This, of course, requires more money and resources."

Vancouver's experience, he said, shows they would be money and resources wisely spent. "Most of the original fear and controversy over this has gone away here," he continued. "I would think this would also be a good idea in U.S. cities that need it, too."

The United States' Ban on Needle Exchange Programs Is Contributing to the Spread of HIV/AIDS

James E. Loyce Jr., Adrian Tyler, and Malik Russell

With the rise in HIV/AIDS that has resulted from intravenous drug use, harm reduction advocates are frustrated by the United States government's refusal to support needle exchange programs. Providing clean needles and treatment for injection drug users would save lives, argue the authors of the following viewpoint. The ban Congress has placed on funding for needle exchange programs is no longer rational, and it is, in fact, contributing to the spread of HIV/AIDS. James E. Loyce Jr. and Adrian Tyler, members of the Black Coalition on AIDS in San Francisco, have partnered with Malik Russell from the Harm Reduction Coalition to write the following commentary.

As you read, consider the following questions:

1. How many new cases of HIV/AIDS per year in the United States can be attributed to intravenous drug use?
2. By what percentage did HIV rates change annually in cities operating needle exchange programs?
3. Why do some people see needle exchange programs as a minority issue?

James E. Loyce Jr., Adrian Tyler, Malik Russell, "U.S. Needle Policy Hurts AIDS Sufferers," *The San Francisco Chronicle*, February 7, 2008, p. B7. http://sfgate.com. Reproduced by permission of the authors.

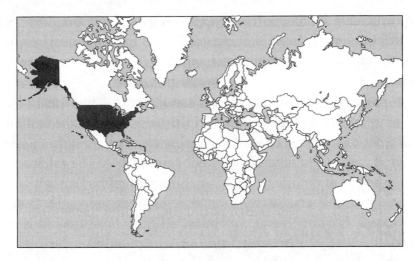

Today [February 7, 2008], the African American community will gather under the banner of National Black HIV/AIDS Awareness Day to bring attention to this modern plague and its disparate impact on the black community.

While HIV/AIDS decimates our community, our nation has failed to implement a national health policy that addresses how this disease is spread. Nowhere is this discrepancy as great as over the issue of needle exchange.

"If most Americans knew ... that we could reduce the spread of HIV/AIDS in the United States by up to one-third, they would run to their congressional representative's office and demand answers."

Needle exchange remains a scientifically proven strategy to curb the spread of AIDS by providing clean needles and access to treatment for injection drug users. Unfortunately, for nearly 20 years Congress has maintained a no-longer-rational ban on the use of federal dollars for needle exchange programs. Congress thinks differently than health professionals and organizations such as the Black AIDS Institute, National Minority AIDS Council, NAACP [National Association for the

Advancement of Colored People], National Urban League, American Academy of Pediatrics, American Bar Association, American Medical Association and U.S. Conference of Mayors.

These groups see needle exchange as a viable means of slowing the spread of the virus. Nearly a quarter of the annual 40,000 new cases of HIV/AIDS in this country are either a direct or collateral effect of intravenous drug use. The failure to have access to clean needles has wide-ranging implications not just for drug users, but also for their families and entire communities. Up to 75 percent of new AIDS cases among women and children are directly or indirectly a consequence of intravenous drug use.

Proven Strategy Is Disregarded

If most Americans knew, by simply removing a political plank in congressional appropriation bills, that we could reduce the spread of HIV/AIDS in the United States by up to one-third, they would run to their congressional representative's office and demand answers. They would want to know why our elected officials ignored a proven strategy to prevent the spread of HIV—a strategy that has already been approved by 16 counties and four cities in California, as well as in more than 20 nations from Europe to Canada.

Due to the federal ban on syringe exchange enacted in 1988, states and cities have been limited to using scarce local funds to combat the damage that results from intravenous drug users sharing HIV-infected needles.

According to the Harm Reduction Coalition, more than 200 needle exchange programs exist in 36 states, and their impact on reducing the spread of HIV and hepatitis C has been amazing. According to a 2005 study of New York City HIV trends, the number of HIV positive injection drug users dropped more than 75 percent from 1990 to 2001. Similarly, a 1997 study in the *Lancet* medical journal compared HIV infection rates among injection drug users in 81 cities around the world. In the 52 cities without needle exchange programs, the rates increased on average 5.9 percent annually; yet in those 29 cities with needle exchange programs, HIV rates dropped 5.8 percent annually.

Health experts have called for allowing federal dollars for needle exchange programs. Advocates for removal of the federal ban cheered when Congress voted to allow the District of Columbia to use its own funds to support syringe exchange programs. In California, Gov. Arnold Schwarzenegger signed into law similar legislation that, after 20 years, finally provides local jurisdictions greater autonomy in using funds to support syringe exchange.

Countless studies have documented the benefit syringe exchange programs have had on reducing HIV/AIDS rates across the globe and here in California, which hosts 39 syringe exchange programs.

Sadly, for African American and Latino communities, the problem of HIV/AIDS has already reached the crisis level. Today, African Americans make up only 12 percent of the national population but the majority of new AIDS cases. Additionally, African Americans make up 50 percent of AIDS cases attributed to drug injection use, while Latinos make up 25 percent.

These horrific numbers could lead many to see the federal ban on syringe exchange programs simply as a "minority" issue instead of the national public health policy issue that it is.

As law professor Lani Guinier noted, America's minority communities often serve as "the canary in the coal mine" for social maladies. Why would health problems facing these communities not eventually impact each and every neighborhood? Already reports from the CDC [Centers for Disease Control and Prevention] indicate that yearly HIV/AIDS infection rates could actually be 20 percent to 50 percent higher than previously estimated.

The Syringe Access Solution

Expanding syringe access requires responses from community members, legislators, service providers, and public health officials. The Centers for Disease Control and Prevention recommend using a new, sterile syringe for each injection. Health jurisdictions across the nation should strive to meet this recommendation by authorizing widespread sterile syringe access programs and over-the-counter pharmacy sales.

A Comprehensive Approach:

- Passing legislation to authorize sterile syringe access

- Confronting the stigmatization of drug use, people who use drugs, and addiction

- Promoting harm reduction and public health measures to address hepatitis C, overdose, and drug dependence

- Addressing and negotiating issues of race, ethnicity, culture, gender, sexual orientation, age, socioeconomic status in the context of disease prevention and harm reduction

Syringe exchange programs are highly cost-effective. The lifetime cost of medical care for each new HIV infection is $385,200; the equivalent amount of money spent on syringe exchange programs would prevent at least 30 new HIV infections.

Harm Reduction Coalition (HRC),
"The Solution," 2008. www.harmreduction.org.

On National Black HIV/AIDS Awareness Day, ours is not a call from the African American community alone. It is a call from advocates the world over, whose communities are plagued by an epidemic and who seek resources for the fight.

Removing the federal ban on syringe exchange programs makes sense economically, politically and morally. Better public policy must not be strangled by Beltway [Washington, D.C.] politics—after all, we are talking about people's lives.

Australia Will Not Benefit from Harm Reduction

Don Weatherburn

Don Weatherburn is the director of the New South Wales Bureau of Crime Statistics and Research in Australia. In the following viewpoint, he argues against harm minimization/harm reduction policies, maintaining that they confuse the public and could lead to increased drug use. This strategy evades real problems, he argues, and Australia should focus on reducing specific drug-related problems instead, such as heroin-related crime and fatal overdoses. In addition to working for the Bureau, Weatherburn is an adjunct professor with the School of Social Science and Policy at the University of New South Wales and is the author of two books.

As you read, consider the following questions:

1. According to Weatherburn, what often happens when the price of an illicit drug increases?
2. What makes demand reduction so appealing to public health advocates, as explained by Weatherburn?
3. According to the author, what would happen if drug use or possession did not carry criminal sanctions and supervised injection centers were set up everywhere?

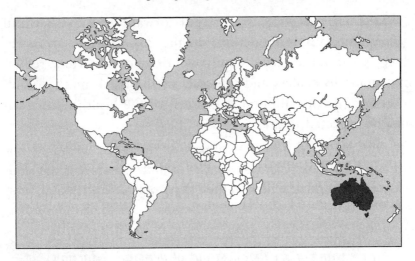

When it comes to illicit drugs, the goal of harm minimisation seems sensible enough, perhaps even trite. But whose harm are we trying to minimise and how do we compare different types of harm? Is it possible to compare the harm done by injecting drug users when they discard needles in a public park with the harm done to injecting drug users when they are unfairly harassed by the police?

It used to be thought that if efforts to reduce the supply of heroin ever succeeded, this would push up prices and force users to commit more crime to fund their addictions.

Thanks to the heroin shortage we now know that pushing up the price of heroin substantially reduces consumption. Higher prices produced a fall in heroin-related crime and fatal overdoses. Police would argue that it also produced a big improvement in public amenity in places like Cabramatta [suburb in New South Wales, Australia].

But reducing the supply of heroin increased some types of harm. The risk we take when we push up the price of one illicit drug is that consumers will switch to another. Evidence is now emerging that the heroin shortage may have increased the demand for methamphetamine and cocaine.

Demand reduction is often put forward as a less harmful policy than supply reduction, on the grounds that if we reduce demand, the excess supply will drive down prices, reducing profits to dealers and the scale of the black market. And, of course, if consumption falls, most of the health harms can also be expected to fall.

One of the things that makes demand reduction so appealing to public health advocates is that its symbols are doctors, nurses and teachers, rather than police, courts and prisons.

"If we want to get the most out of demand reduction . . . we have to inflict some harm."

But let's think about what drives drug users into treatment. Some experience an epiphany and go voluntarily but many are like Tom Waits in the song *Bad Liver and a Broken Heart*, in which he said he didn't have a drinking problem except when he couldn't get a drink. People who try heroin, cocaine or amphetamines are not generally prompted to stop using because of adverse pharmacological effects.

The most common reasons given by injecting drug users for entering treatment are trouble with police, the cost of drugs and the lifestyle associated with dependence—endless scamming, theft, violence and risk of imprisonment. To maximise the attractions of treatment it helps to make life without it fairly unpleasant. If we want to get the most out of demand reduction, in other words, we have to inflict some harm.

Some argue we should concentrate on reducing the harm suffered by drug users rather than reducing drug use.

The two best-known examples of this strategy are the needle and syringe program and the medically supervised injection centre in Kings Cross [in New South Wales, Australia]. There is no evidence that either of these initiatives have caused any harm. But part of the difficulty in evaluating the harm reduction as a general policy is that we really just tinker at the margins.

Harm Minimisation Is Not a Needed Goal

If you doubt this, just think for a minute about what you could do if you were really serious about limiting the harm illegal drugs do to those who use them.

We could remove criminal sanctions altogether from personal drug use or possession so drug users would not end up with a criminal record and find their career prospects ruined.

To avoid compromising the education of schoolchildren, we could adopt a policy of not expelling students caught with drugs. We could establish a medically supervised injection centre in every neighbourhood.

Why don't we do these things? The most commonly heard reason is that we will ultimately end up with more users and higher levels of harm. It is customary in some circles to scoff at this argument, but it may not be quite as silly as it sounds. Our policies towards alcohol and tobacco rely heavily on stigmatisation and measures designed to increase the cost of use.

Harm minimisation was from its inception less a policy goal than a political fix, designed to ensure that illicit drug use was not viewed solely through the prism of law enforcement.

Harm minimisation might be a worthy goal in the United States, which still places too much emphasis on drug law enforcement and not enough on treatment. Australia, though, no longer needs the goal of harm minimisation.

All it really does is confuse the public and gloss over tensions in drug policy that are better brought to the surface and debated.

Everything we do in the name of drug policy carries risks, costs and benefits. They cannot be added up in a way that would tell us what policy best minimises drug-related harm.

Trends in Non-Fatal Overdose, New South Wales and Cabramatta, Australia

Overdoses and robberies both decreased over time when the supply of heroin was reduced.

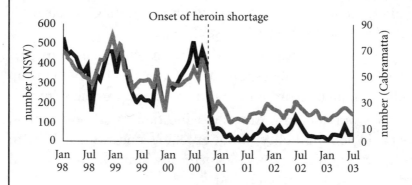

Trends in Robbery, New South Wales and Cabramatta, Australia

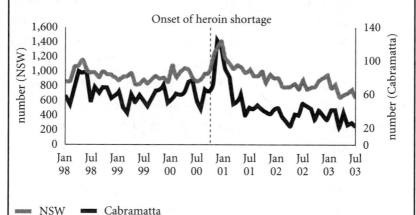

NSW   Cabramatta

TAKEN FROM: Neil Donnelly, Don Weatherburn, and Marilyn Chilvers, "The Impact of the Australian Heroin Shortage on Robbery in New South Wales," *Crime and Justice Statistics: Bureau Brief*, March 2004.

Instead of committing ourselves to harm minimisation we would be better off simply listing specific problems we wish to reduce, such as heroin-related crime, fatal heroin overdoses, hepatitis C and amphetamine psychosis.

Then we can have an open and frank debate about what harms, risks and benefits matter the most.

The United Kingdom's Obsession with Criminalization Maximizes Harm

Danny Kushlick

In the following viewpoint, author Danny Kushlick outlines the shortcomings of the United Kingdom's illegal drug policy. He explains that the current policy focusing on crime ignores and increases the greater problem of public health, and a widespread lack of study and understanding prevents policy makers from seeing the facts. This largely leads to the punishment of a social class that is already disadvantaged. Danny Kushlick is the spokesperson for the Drugs and Health Alliance (DHA), a group of organizations that support evidence-based public health approaches to drug problems.

As you read, consider the following questions:

1. As Kushlick indicates, why is the United Kingdom's current drug policy at odds with social and legislative norms?

2. How has an obsession with reducing crime created harm for drug addicts, according to Kushlick?

3. How does drug use differ between the Netherlands and the United Kingdom?

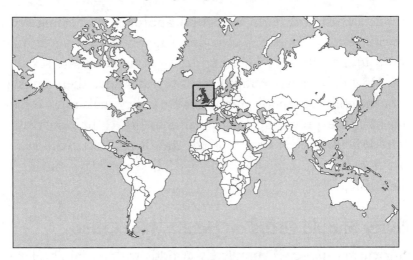

UK [United Kingdom] drug policy is unique. In no other area of social policy do we criminalise at one stroke both recreation and disadvantage. In no other area have we seen so much evidence of the counterproductive effects of a predominantly criminal justice response to a public health problem. And we have seen almost no genuine debate or evidence-based scrutiny from ministers. The last 10 years of this parliament's tacit and active support for a policy based on moral panic has finally broken the camel's back. As the Home Office reviews its last 10-year strategy—results are expected next month—the Drugs and Health Alliance has been formed to bring together organisations committed to bringing about a public health-led approach for the next decade.

"Throughout the last decade government has shown a pathological unwillingness to debate the efficacy of the current approach [to the drug problem]."

In the mid-80s the Conservative government, in the face of a potential HIV/AIDS epidemic, initiated a proactive harm reduction strategy that led to the UK having one of the world's lowest rates of HIV. It was based exclusively on a pragmatic public health and harm reduction approach to dealing with unsafe sex and injecting. No one suggested that we should ramp up penalties for injecting drugs or make unsafe sex illegal. How times have changed. Twenty years later there are significant political taboos among senior policy makers who dare question the prevailing tough criminal justice line on drugs. The result has been that most of the drugs initiatives in the last decade have had draconian [strict, severe] law-making at their core.

Policy Should Focus on Health, Not Crime

Our current policy is completely at odds with social and legislative norms, a strategy based on criminalising drugs in order to reduce social harm. Yet, as the PM's [prime minister] strategy unit drugs report of 2003 showed, it is the very illegality of the supply and use of drugs that causes harm. Despite our commitment to harm reduction, drug use exists within a political and legal framework that is harm maximising; hepatitis C remains at 80% among injecting drug-users and HIV, while still very low, is on the increase.

Throughout the last decade government has shown a pathological unwillingness to debate the efficacy of the current approach. Witness the lack of genuine engagement with the Police Foundation drugs report of 2000, the Home Affairs Select Committee report of 2002, the Science and Technology Committee report on drug classification of 2006 and the recent RSA [Royal Society for the Encouragement of Arts, Manufacture & Commerce] report, as well as the announced and then withdrawn public consultation on the drug classification system and the lack of consultation or parliamentary scrutiny of the Drugs Act 2005. The list is endless. One concern is that the upcoming consultation on the future of the UK drug strategy will end up looking strikingly similar to the last one.

'Drug Misuse Research Institute,' cartoon by Fran. CartoonStock.com.

The frustration of many working in the drugs field is that the obsession with crime reduction has overshadowed the need for improvement of individual and public health. We are demonising some of the most marginalised people in the UK rather than offering them effective treatment. For commissioners of services, this ought to look perverse and bizarre: enforce the drug laws in such a way as to increase the offending of problematic users of the most dangerous drugs, "identify" them through the criminal justice system and finally spend money on "treatment", as ordered by the court, as a way of reducing their offending. The £13bn to £16bn [British pounds, billion] in crime costs associated with the current drug policy should suggest an urgent reallocation of the billions spent on counterproductive heavy-handed enforcement, toward education, dealing with underlying social problems and treatment in a primary care setting.

Ultimately, we need a new paradigm for drug policy development, one based around health and well-being rather than macho posturing and knee-jerk, short-term responses to the failures of the current criminal justice-based policy. The UK sits atop the rankings for levels of problematic heroin and cocaine use. The Dutch, Spanish, Swiss, Portuguese and numerous other nations have all adopted a more public health-focused approach. The average age of heroin users in the Netherlands is 40. They have half the rate of cannabis use compared to the UK. Isn't it time that we joined them?

The consultation on the new strategy offers a window of opportunity for change that will close again soon. This is our chance to let government know that tough enforcement does not reduce harm, it creates it. We should grab the chance with both hands.

Sweden's Zero-Tolerance Policy Is a Good Model for Scotland

Gillian Bowditch

While prohibition has continually failed throughout the world, Sweden has managed to retain one of the lowest drug use rates by enforcing its strict anti-drugs policy—with an astonishingly low 12 percent of the adult population having ever tried illicit drugs. Though many Europeans view Sweden's zero-tolerance approach as harsh and impractical, London's Sunday Times *writer Gillian Bowditch argues that it would be a better model for Scotland and might help reduce drug abuse related deaths, which rose 25 percent in 2006. Sweden's policy is so effective because it focuses on health, argues Bowditch, with obligatory treatment given to addicts. However, such treatment is very different from Scotland's current harm reduction strategy, wherein users give up one drug only to become addicted to another.*

As you read, consider the following questions:

1. Why is an abolitionist policy effective in Sweden?

2. How did a former 1965 prescription-based policy fail in Sweden?

3. How has the methadone program performed in Scotland?

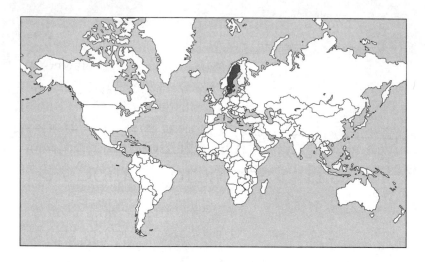

As far as national stereotypes go, the French may be iras-
cible, the Italians volatile and the Scots parsimonious, but
Sweden has long been considered a permissive society. It is an
image bolstered by dodgy 1970s films and the bedroom antics
of [Swedish television presenter] Ulrika Jonsson and [swedish
football manager] Sven-Goran Erickson [known for their
Scandalous affair]. So when Scotland is urged to adopt "the
Swedish model", a vision of a blonde au pair [young, foreign
nanny] in hot pants is the first thing that springs to mind.

When it comes to drugs, however, Sweden has the most
draconian [strict] policy in Europe, with compulsory treatment orders for addicts and harsh jail sentences for possession. It's a zero-tolerance approach rejected by the rest of Europe as unrealistic. But evidence suggests it works. Now
Swedish politicians, horrified at the extent of Scotland's drug
culture, are urging MSPs [Members of Scottish Parliament] to
follow their lead.

There are fewer drug deaths in the whole of Sweden than
there are in Glasgow. A delegation of 15 Swedish politicians
and civil servants visited Scotland last month [October 2007].
According to Tomas Hallberg, director of European Cities
Against Drugs, what they saw horrified them.

"Just walking the streets of Glasgow was very shocking for them, to see the drugs problem so open and obvious. You are on the edge and if you don't do anything about it, it will be very, very difficult to turn this ocean liner round."

Concerns about the drug crisis come in a week when it was revealed that Scotland was becoming a manufacturer of drugs as well as a consumer. Police believe up to £1 billion [British pounds] worth of cannabis is being cultivated every year by organised gangs. In the past year, 61 cannabis factories have been raided in Strathclyde [region in southwestern Scotland] alone. Stephen House, the chief constable of Strathclyde police, has vowed to make drug-related crime a priority.

Sweden has only 28,000 drug users among its population of 9m [million] people. The 2007 International Narcotics Control Strategy Report notes that drug use in Sweden is a third of the European average, with only 12% of the adult population having ever used drugs. Last year, the number of serious drug users fell 7% and the percentage of high school students who have tried drugs also dropped.

By contrast Scotland has more than 50,000 heroin addicts—the figure for drug users is significantly higher—in a population of just over 5m.

Scottish deaths linked to drug abuse rose 25% to 421 last year and drug use among young people is steadily increasing.

It's fashionable to view drug abuse as an intractable problem beyond the remit of politicians. But Antonio Maria Costa, executive director of the UN [United Nation] Office on Drugs and Crime, says Scotland's drug crisis can be blamed on failed government policies.

"The achievements of Sweden are proof that, ultimately, each government is responsible for the size of the drug problem in its country," he says.

Professor Neil McKeganey, of Glasgow University's Centre for Drug Misuse Research, believes Scotland would do well to examine the Swedish approach. Although Nicola Sturgeon, the health secretary, announced a £25m package for addiction treatment last week, the Scottish National party's focus has been on alcohol abuse. While McKeganey welcomes the tough approach on alcohol, he is worried the party does not have a coherent strategy on drugs.

"I cannot remember the last public statement from the Nationalists on drugs," he says. "I think that is a concern because it comes quite close to a sense of drift.

"If somebody asked me what the Nationalists' policy on drugs is, I'd have to say 'I don't know'.

"I would like to see an unequivocal policy which says we should aim to remove the drug problem from society. All our interventions should aim to do that. When one starts to entertain notions that one can accommodate the drug problem and provide services with a view to reducing the harm associated with continued drug use, you enter a confusing realm."

The abolitionist policy, which many drug workers and law enforcers believe is unworkable, is the reason Swedish policy is so effective, according to Maria Larsson, Sweden's minister for public health. "The vision is that of a society free from narcotic drugs," she says. "People are entitled to a life of dignity and a society that safeguards health, prosperity, security and safety of the individual."

"There is very big support for a zero-tolerance policy. More than 94% of adults support zero tolerance as do 92% of young people."

A Grassroots Model

So what exactly makes Sweden's drug policy so successful? "You have to start with the basics," says Hallberg who, like the rest of the Swedish delegation, paid for the trip to Scotland out of his own pocket.

"You have to have laws that prohibit even a small amount of drugs and these have to be enforced. This has to be supported by prevention work. Society as a whole has to have a united approach to drugs. If all of that fails, you have to offer the individual effective treatment. It costs a lot and needs a lot of coordination between different authorities.

"The Swedish model is built on a people's movement. It comes from a grassroots level. People have forced the government to create the policy we have today. There is very big support for a zero-tolerance policy. More than 94% of adults support zero tolerance as do 92% of young people, so it's quite easy to uphold."

Sweden has not always taken such a hard line. The country had a serious problem with drugs in the 1930s when there was a fashion for taking amphetamines. Then, in 1965, a disastrous experimental policy was introduced, allowing doctors to prescribe opiates and amphetamines. The policy worked on the basis of supply and demand.

These drugs spread into the black market and the addiction problem grew. Detective Superintendent Eva Brannmark of the National Police Board of Sweden remembers the consequences. It is a lesson for those who advocate the prescription of heroin on the National Health Service. "I was then working at the Solna police authority, which is now part of the Stockholm county police authority," she says. "We had three known abusers in our area who lived in one-room apartments. They knew us, we knew them and we used to visit them in their homes. The situation changed dramatically soon after the trials started. There were sometimes 10 to 20 people, all under the influence of drugs, and plenty of illegally prescribed drugs in these apartments, and there was nothing we could do.

"A few months later, there were hundreds of abusers in the area and the police had totally lost control."

Shaken by the death of a 17-year-old woman from an overdose of morphine and amphetamine that had been procured through the project, the Swedes started to take a more evidence-based approach to the problem. The strategy was guided by Nils Bejerot, a deputy social medical officer at the child and youth welfare board of the city of Stockholm.

Bejerot established the Association for a Drug-Free Society, which played an important role in shaping policy. He warned of the consequences of an "epidemic of addiction".

"In Sweden half the addicts receive in-patient treatment; in Scotland it is less than 1%."

As a result, there was a progressive tightening of Swedish drug laws from 1968 onwards. While the rest of Europe was hanging out, the Swedes were adopting a 10-point plan and raising the jail term for dealers. By 1980, when Scotland was beginning to experience a heroin problem, the Swedes were getting tough. Only those in possession of minuscule quantities of drugs could escape prosecution. By 1982 addicts could be coerced into treatment against their will and by 1993 even low-level drug use was an imprisonable offence.

Drug Use Seen as a Moral Issue

Scotland, meanwhile, has developed a smorgasbord of policies, not all of which have been rigorously evaluated. The most controversial is the methadone programme, which according to McKeganey has largely been a waste of money.

"The residential rehabilitation services are seven times more likely to bring someone to a drug-free state than any other service, yet these services are the least available," he says.

"I think it is scandalous that we have 22,000 addicts on methadone. We can have people on methadone for 15 years and they are not substantially better off at the end of that than when they started. They are simply more dependent on another drug.

"Over 10 years, according to the Scottish government's figures, we have spent £100m on methadone. Where do you see the benefits of that massive investment?

"One big difference between the Scottish and Swedish approaches is that, in Sweden, drug use is considered morally reprehensible."

"We have put so much emphasis into getting addicts into treatment—which is what targets and performance indicators are geared to—that the only treatment that can accommodate them is giving them a drug. Outcome measures are woeful and they aren't geared to the predominant treatment we are offering. In Sweden half the addicts receive in-patient treatment; in Scotland it is less than 1%."

One big difference between the Scottish and Swedish approaches is that, in Sweden, drug use is considered morally reprehensible. In Britain, middle-class cocaine and cannabis use is seen as neutral.

"Drug use is less acceptable at all levels of society here," says Hallberg. "It's a moral issue, but we are not moralising about drug addicts. Our philosophy is that it should be difficult to take drugs, but easy to get treatment. In many ways addicts are treated very well. Compulsory treatment is an element of our policy, but only if an addict is refusing to go into rehab. It's a last resort."

Hallberg, who visited the Scottish parliament, is so concerned about the country's problem that he has extended an offer to any Scottish city wanting to join his network. "I would personally guarantee they will have the facilities they need to see us in Sweden and Stockholm. They can come and learn from us at any time."

"What is needed is a commitment across political parties to address this issue and suspend the political point-scoring," says McKeganey. "The way in which we have to tackle the

The Role of Nils Bejerot in Shaping Swedish Drug Control Policy

The theoretical foundation of Sweden's restrictive drug policy of the 1970s and 1980s appears to be largely based on the work of Nils Bejerot, who is sometimes referred to as the founding father of Swedish drug control policy. A deputy social medical officer at the Child and Youth Welfare Board of the City of Stockholm, Bejerot diagnosed first cases of juvenile intravenous drug use in Stockholm in 1954, much earlier than in most other towns in Europe.

In 1965, Bejerot initiated a study at the Stockholm Remand Prison to monitor the spread of intravenous drug abuse in Stockholm, which confirmed his scepticism of the consequences of legally prescribing amphetamine to amphetamine users.

In 1969, Bejerot founded the 'Association for a Drug-Free Society' (RNS), which played an important role in shaping Swedish drug policies. He warned of the consequences of an 'epidemic addiction', prompted by young, psychologically and socially unstable persons who, usually after direct personal initiation from another drug abuser, begin to use socially non-accepted, intoxicating drugs to gain euphoria. . . .

The practical [policy] implications [of his ideas]—which over the years were put into practice—were: (i) to increase prevention and treatment activities as well as to criminalize not only drug trafficking but also drug use, (ii) to target cannabis use as the first drug in the chain towards drug abuse (based on the 'gateway'/'stepping stone' hypotheses) and (iii) to create a national consensus on drug policies across party lines, supported by civil society pressure groups.

United Nations Office on Drugs and Crime, "Sweden's Successful Drug Policy: A Review of the Evidence," February 2007.

drugs problem is similar to the way in which we have to tackle terrorism. I don't think that means taking draconian measures against the end user, because that person clearly needs treatment, but we should be uncompromising in other areas. We have become acclimatised to 400 young people dead every year.

"It is an incredible haemorrhaging of young life out of Scotland. Drugs are leaching so much from society. If you go to parts of the east end of Glasgow, it is like going to another country."

Sadly, that country isn't Sweden.

Periodical Bibliography

The following articles have been selected to supplement the diverse views presented in this chapter.

BBC News   "Call for Drugs 'Injecting Rooms,'" May 30, 2008. http://news.bbc.co.uk.

Bob Curley   "Critics Say Health Plans Put Lives at Risk by Requiring Prior Approval for Buprenorphine," *Join Together*, May 16, 2008. www.jointogether .org.

Harm Reduction Coalition   "Syringe Exchange in Prisons: The International Experience," January 2007. www.harm reduction.org.

Am Johal   "Drug War Clashes with Fight Against HIV/ AIDS," Inter Press Service (IPS), October 3, 2007.

The Kiwi Party Press Release   "Harm Minimization Not Working, Government Living in Dream World," *Scoop Independent News*, May 29, 2008. www.scoop.co.nz.

Rod Mickleburgh   "Safe-Injection Site in B.C. Wins Court Protection," *The Globe and Mail*, May 27, 2008. www .theglobeandmail.com.

Bill Piper and Naomi Long   "A Shot at Curbing the AIDS Epidemic," *The Washington Post*, January 27, 2008. www.wash ingtonpost.com.

Peter Reuter and Harold Pollack   "How Much Can Treatment Reduce National Drug Problems?" *Addiction*, vol. 101, 2006, pp. 341–347.

Daniel Wolfe   "Harsh Treatment," *International Herald Tribune*, December 27, 2006. www.iht.com.

For Further Discussion

Chapter 1

1. Ethan Nadelmann contends that the United States, with its failed policies of prohibition, should not serve as a role model for international drug policy, even though the country has "dominated the drug control agencies of the United Nations and other international organizations" for many years. After reading the other viewpoints in this chapter, do you think that this a fair assessment? Which viewpoints support Nadelmann's argument? Has the United States achieved any favorable results through its influence and intervention?

2. Some of the material in the chapter suggests that the war on drugs has indirectly empowered paramilitary groups, thus undermining weak governments. How and why has this happened? What are some possible solutions to counteract this problem?

Chapter 2

1. Many of the authors in this chapter point to the failures and damaging consequences of prohibition, arguing that such measures have failed to curb the flow of drugs. Considering all of the eradication efforts to destroy illicit drug crops, such as coca in Colombia and poppies in Afghanistan, along with all of the United States' interdiction efforts, such as cocaine seizures and domestic meth lab raids, how is it possible that drugs are still being produced faster and cheaper? Why is prohibition not working?

Chapter 3

1. While the production of illegal drugs has led to environmental degradation, fighting the war on drugs has also presented damage to the environment. Which do you think poses a greater threat and why? Do you believe that there is adequate justification for the United States to continue its aerial fumigation programs?

Chapter 4

1. Kailash Chand argues that prohibition in the United Kingdom has increased the dangers of substance abuse and that decriminalization would reduce drug addiction. In contrast, Joseph A. Califano Jr. contends that prohibition is protecting individuals and society from the harms of drug addiction and that decriminalization would be dangerous, making illicit drugs more acceptable and easier to obtain. Which argument do you find more convincing? Why?

2. Why do you think a policy of liberal decriminalization has succeeded in the Netherlands? Given Andrew Stuttaford's remark that Amsterdam has become a tourist attraction, of sorts, "a druggy destination overwhelmed by day trippers . . . cannabis kitsch, and counterculture dreck—which could end up destroying the typically civil Dutch compromise that has made [decriminalization] possible," do you think liberal decriminalization could work in the United States? Why or why not?

Chapter 5

1. Theodore Dalrymple argues that harm reduction policies are "inherently infantilizing" since addicts are not held accountable for their problems with drug abuse. The responsibility for the addict's recovery is misplaced, he maintains, and authorities are to blame for the consequences. Other viewpoints in the chapter positively sup-

port harm reduction and point out that the approach saves lives and helps addicts recover. Do you agree or disagree with Dalrymple's argument? Why? In the case of Insite, the Canadian supervised injection facility, do you feel that addicts treated there are held accountable for their consequences? Why or why not?

2. Danny Kushlick believes that criminalization has led to increased drug related harm in the United Kingdom. "We are demonising some of the most marginalised people," he argues, "rather than offering them effective treatment." Do you find this to be the case in other countries as well? What about in the United States? Why or why not? Defend your answer with evidence presented in other chapter viewpoints.

Organizations to Contact

The editors have compiled the following list of organizations concerned with the issues debated in this book. The descriptions are derived from materials provided by the organizations. All have publications or information available for interested readers. The list was compiled on the date of publication of the present volume; the information provided here may change. Readers need to remember that many organizations take several weeks or longer to respond to inquiries.

American Council for Drug Education (ACDE)
Phoenix House, American Council for Drug Education
164 W. Seventy-Fourth Street, New York, NY   10023
(800) 488-DRUG
e-mail: acde@phoenixhouse.org
Web site: www.acde.org

Working under its parent company, Phoenix House, the American Council for Drug Education (ACDE) is an agency dedicated to educating the public about substance abuse. The organization provides authoritative information on tobacco, alcohol, and drugs to health care professionals, employers, policy makers, the media, educators, parents, and young adults. The agency distributes a variety of information, including fact sheets, pamphlets, brochures, books, videos, and teaching aids for educators such as lesson plans for the classroom.

Canadian Foundation for Drug Policy (CFDP)
70 MacDonald Street, Ottawa, Ontario   K2P 1H6
   Canada
(613) 236-1027 • fax: (613) 238-2891
e-mail: eoscapel@cfdp.ca
Web site: www.cfdp.ca

A nonprofit organization launched in 1993, the Canadian Foundation for Drug Policy (CFDP) was founded by a team of Canada's leading drug policy experts including lawyers, psychologists, pharmacologists, and policy advocates and researchers. The foundation serves as a channel between the government, other organizations, the media, and the public. The foundation distributes a variety of information through its Web site, including articles on drug policy, educational materials, and background information on drug laws.

Drug Enforcement Administration (DEA)
Mailstop: AES, 2401 Jefferson Davis Highway
Alexandria, VA 22301
(202) 307-1000
Web site: www.usdoj.gov/dea

The Drug Enforcement Administration (DEA) is the United States' federal agency tasked with enforcing controlled substances laws and regulations. The DEA is also responsible for coordinating U.S. drug investigations internationally. The DEA investigates drug-related criminal activity, manages a national drug intelligence program, and carries out seizures of drugs and assets related to drug trafficking. The DEA publishes a variety of reports, leaflets, and educational materials and maintains a large online multimedia library. The DEA also maintains www.justthinktwice.com, an educational Web site for teens dedicated to preventing drug abuse.

Drug Policy Alliance Network (DPAN)
70 W. Thirty-Sixth Street, 16th Floor, New York, NY 10018
(212) 613-8020 • fax: (212) 613-8021
e-mail: nyc@drugpolicy.org
Web site: www.drugpolicy.org

The Drug Policy Alliance Network (DPAN) is the leading organization in the United States working toward drug policy reform; with a heavy emphasis on health and human rights, the organization promotes harm reduction to minimize the dangers of drug abuse and prohibition. DPAN is actively engaged in education and lobbying, and apart from undertaking many projects and drug policy reform initiatives in the United States, the organization also supports reform efforts across the

239

globe, particularly in Europe, Australia, and the Americas. The organization publishes many reports, articles, and booklets; in addition, the Drug Policy Alliance (DPA), a partner organization of DPAN, maintains the Lindesmith Library in New York, one of the world's leading resources for drug-related information, which houses over fifteen thousand books, documents, and videos, as well as an online library of electronic materials.

European Monitoring Centre for Drugs and Drug Addiction (EMCDDA)
Rua da Cruz de Santa Apolónia 23–25
Lisbon   1149-045 PT
351-218113000 • fax: 351-218131711
e-mail: info@emcdda.europa.eu
Web site: www.emcdda.europa.eu

The European Monitoring Centre for Drugs and Drug Addiction (EMCDDA) is the central source of information on drugs and drug addiction in the European Union. The organization works to improve the comparability of drug information and to provide policy makers with a framework of reliable evidence used to analyze and develop drug laws. The EMCDDA works with roughly thirty national monitoring centers to gather and analyze data and operates Best Practice Portal, an online research resource used by professionals in the field, as well as the European Legal Database on Drugs (ELDD), an online database housing drug legislation information. The EMCDDA publishes *Drugnet Europe*, a newsletter issued four times per year; *Drugs in Focus*, a series of policy briefings; "Insights," a series covering research carried out by the agency; "Monographs," special publications containing scientific papers; and other brochures and leaflets.

Harm Reduction Coalition (HRC)
22 W. Twenty-Seventh Street, 5th Floor
New York, NY   10001
(212) 213-6376 • fax: (212) 213-6582
e-mail: hrc@harmreduction.org
Web site: www.harmreduction.org

The Harm Reduction Coalition (HRC) is a national organization that encourages support for the health and well-being of people impacted by drug use. The organization backs harm reduction policies and programs that help minimize the dangers of drug use, including addiction, overdose, and diseases easily spread by drug-injecting users, such as HIV and hepatitis C. The HRC gives special emphasis to areas where inequalities and social injustice intensify drug-related harms. The coalition also actively promotes syringe access. HRC offers a variety of services and programs; moreover, its Harm Reduction Training Institute (HRTI) provides training and education to care providers working within drug-using populations. Fact sheets, briefings, and a variety of other educational materials are available on the organization's Web site.

International Harm Reduction Association (IHRA)
Unit 704, The Chandlery, 50 Westminster Bridge Road
London   SE1 7QY   England
44-02079537412
e-mail: info@ihra.net
Web site: www.ihra.net

An international, not-for-profit, nongovernmental organization, the International Harm Reduction Association (IHRA) is the leading association promoting harm reduction on a global basis to prevent the negative consequences of illicit drugs, alcohol, and tobacco for individuals and society. IHRA supports reducing harm and protecting human rights within national, regional, and international bodies such as the United Nations. IHRA is actively involved in conferences, advocacy and campaigns, research, and communications. The association disseminates information and educational materials through its Web site, including papers, documents, and articles written by IHRA and other authors—most can be downloaded directly from the site or through links to external Web sites. The association also publishes the *International Journal of Drug Policy* (*IJDP*), the official journal of the IHRA that explores current research and analysis on drug use and policy on a global scale.

RAND
1776 Main Street, PO Box 2138
Santa Monica, CA   90407-2138
(310) 393-0411 • fax: (310) 393-4818
Web site: www.rand.org

The RAND Corporation is a nonprofit institution focused on issues such as national security, law, education, business, health, and science. The institution works to improve public policy through research and analysis—to help address complex questions deliberated in the United States and around the globe. Since 1989, RAND's Drug Policy Research Center (DPRC) has offered policy makers objective research and provided a solid foundation for dealing with drug-abuse related problems. RAND publishes a substantial array of material, including articles, reports, and books. The Drug Policy Research Center publishes *DPRC Insights*, an electronic newsletter, in addition to an extensive collection of substance abuse research.

Transform Drug Policy Foundation (TDPF)
Easton Business Centre, Felix Road, Bristol   BS5 0HE
    United Kingdom
44-01179415810 • fax: 44-01179415809
e-mail: info@tdpf.org.uk
Web site: www.tdpf.org.uk

The Transform Drug Policy Foundation (TDPF) is the leading drug policy reform charity in the United Kingdom, working to expand the debate on current UK and international drug policy; the organization promotes alternatives to prohibition and supports harm reduction to restore health and human rights. TDPF works closely with government agencies and law enforcement, political parties, parliamentarians, nongovernmental organizations, scholars, and the media and carries out research and policy analysis. The organization publishes a number of articles, briefings, reports, and leaflets, most available for download on the Web site.

Transnational Institute (TNI)
PO Box 14656, Amsterdam   1001 LD
   The Netherlands
31-206626608 • fax: 31-206757176
e-mail: tni@tni.org
Web site: www.tni.org

The Transnational Institute (TNI) is an international network of activist-scholars dedicated to researching and analyzing global problems. Founded in 1974, its mission is to provide academic support to world conflicts such as war, poverty, human rights violations, and environmental degradation. TNI's Drugs and Democracy Programme promotes policy reform and emphasizes harm reduction principles. TNI publishes reports, debate papers, policy briefings, and monographs. Many publications are available for download via the Web site.

United Nations Office on Drugs & Crime (UNODC)
Vienna International Centre, PO Box 500, Vienna   A 1400
   Austria
43-126060 • fax: 43-12633389
Web site: www.unodc.org

The United Nations Office on Drugs & Crime (UNODC) was established in 1997 through a merger between the United Nations Drug Control Programme and the Centre for International Crime Prevention in an effort to control drug abuse and trafficking. The organization is charged with fighting illegal drugs, crime, and terrorism and operates internationally through a vast network of field offices. UNODC publishes an extensive list of documents including reports and surveys, most of which are available in PDF format for download through the Web site.

Bibliography of Books

Alan W. Bock — *Waiting to Inhale: The Politics of Medical Marijuana*. Santa Ana, CA: Seven Locks Press, 2000.

Julia Buxton — *The Political Economy of Narcotics: Production, Consumption and Global Markets*. London: Zed Books, 2006.

Ted Galen Carpenter — *Bad Neighbor Policy: Washington's Futile War on Drugs in Latin America*. New York: Palgrave MacMillan, 2003.

Benjamin Dangl — *The Price of Fire: Resource Wars and Social Movements in Bolivia*. Oakland, CA: AK Press, 2007.

Richard Davenport-Hines — *The Pursuit of Oblivion: A Global History of Narcotics*. New York: Norton, 2002.

Douglas J. Davids — *Narco-Terrorism: A Unified Strategy to Fight a Growing Terrorist Menace*. Ardsley, NY: Transnational Publishers, 2002.

Patt Denning — *Practicing Harm Reduction Psychotherapy: An Alternative Approach to Addictions*. New York: Guilford Press, 2004.

Frank Dikötter, Lars Laamann et al. — *Narcotic Culture: A History of Drugs in China*. Chicago: University of Chicago Press, 2004.

Sergio Ferragut   *A Silent Nightmare: The Bottom Line and the Challenge of Illicit Drugs.* Reston, VA: S. Ferragut, 2007.

Gary L. Fisher   *Rethinking Our War on Drugs: Candid Talk About Controversial Issues.* Westport, CT: Praeger, 2006.

Laurie Freeman   *State of Siege: Drug-Related Violence and Corruption in Mexico: Unintended Consequences of the War on Drugs.* Washington, DC: Washington Office on Latin America, 2006.

Jurg Gerber and Eric L. Jensen   *Drug War, American Style: The Internationalization of Failed Policy and Its Alternatives.* New York: Garland, 2001.

Rudolph J. Gerber   *Legalizing Marijuana: Drug Policy Reform and Prohibition Politics.* Westport, CT: Praeger, 2004.

James P. Gray   *Why Our Drug Laws Have Failed and What We Can Do About It: A Judicial Indictment of the War on Drugs.* Philadelphia: Temple University Press, 2001.

Mike Gray   *Busted: Stone Cowboys, Narco-Lords, and Washington's War on Drugs.* New York: Thunder's Mouth Press/Nation Books, 2002.

Joel Hafvenstein   *Opium Season: A Year on the Afghan Frontier.* Guilford, CT: Lyons Press, 2007.

M. Emdad-ul Haq — *Drugs in South Asia: From the Opium Trade to the Present Day.* New York: St. Martin's Press, 2000.

Laura E. Huggins — *Drug War Deadlock: The Policy Battle Continues.* Stanford, CA: Hoover Institution Press, Stanford University, 2005.

James A. Inciardi — *The War on Drugs IV: The Continuing Saga of the Mysteries and Miseries of Intoxication, Addiction, Crime, and Public Policy.* Boston: Pearson/Allyn and Bacon, 2008.

Martin Jelsma, Tom Kramer et al. — *Trouble in the Triangle: Opium and Conflict in Burma.* Chiang Mai, Thailand: Silkworm Books, 2005.

Dirk Johnson — *Meth: The Home-Cooked Menace.* Center City, MN: Hazelden, 2005.

Robin Kirk — *More Terrible than Death: Massacres, Drugs, and America's War in Colombia.* New York: Public Affairs, 2003.

Axel Klein, Marcus Day et al. — *Caribbean Drugs: From Criminalization to Harm Reduction.* London: Zed Books, 2004.

Gregory D. Lee — *Conspiracy Investigations: Terrorism, Drugs, and Gangs.* Upper Saddle River, NJ: Pearson Prentice Hall, 2005.

Carl G. Leukefeld, Frank M. Tims et al. — *Treatment of Drug Offenders: Policies and Issues.* New York: Springer Publishing, 2002.

Grace Livingstone *Inside Colombia: Drugs, Democracy and War*. New Brunswick, NJ: Rutgers University Press, 2004.

Dave Macdonald *Drugs in Afghanistan: Opium, Outlaws and Scorpion Tales*. London: Pluto Press, 2007.

David R. Mares *Drug Wars and Coffeehouses: The Political Economy of the International Drug Trade*. Washington, DC: CQ Press, 2006.

Alfred W. McCoy *The Politics of Heroin: CIA Complicity in the Global Drug Trade, Afghanistan, Southeast Asia, Central America, Colombia*. Chicago: Lawrence Hill Books, 2003.

Lee Morgan II *The Reaper's Line: Life and Death on the Mexican Border*. Tucson, AZ: Rio Nuevo Publishers, 2006.

Clayton James Mosher and Scott Akins *Drugs and Drug Policy: The Control of Consciousness Alteration*. Thousand Oaks, CA: Sage, 2007.

Mikki Norris, Chris Conrad et al. *Shattered Lives: Portraits from America's Drug War*. El Cerrito, CA: Creative Xpressions, 2000.

Matthew B. Robinson and Renee G. Scherlen *Lies, Damned Lies, and Drug War Statistics: A Critical Analysis of Claims Made by the Office of National Drug Control Policy*. Albany: State University of New York Press, 2007.

Merrill Singer   *Drugs and Development: Drugging the Poor: Legal and Illegal Drugs and Social Inequality.* Long Grove, IL: Waveland Press, Inc., 2008.

Merrill Singer   *Drugs and Development: The Global Impact on Sustainable Growth and Human Rights.* Long Grove, IL: Waveland Press, Inc., 2008.

Doug Stokes   *America's Other War: Terrorizing Colombia.* London: Zed Books, 2005.

John Strang and Michael Gossop   *Heroin Addiction and the British System.* London: Routledge, 2005.

Andrew Tatarsky   *Harm Reduction Psychotherapy: A New Treatment for Drug and Alcohol Problems.* Lanham, MD: Rowman & Littlefield Publishers, Inc., 2007.

Tim Boekhout van Solinge and Willem Pompe   *Dealing with Drugs in Europe: An Investigation of European Drug Control Experience: France, The Netherlands, and Sweden.* The Hague: Willem Pompe Institute for Criminal Law and Criminology and BJu Legal Publishers, 2004.

Index

Geographic headings and page numbers in **boldface** refer to viewpoints about that country or region.

L

M